D1566790

THE
TRUE GEOGRAPHY
OF OUR COUNTRY

To the Crozet Library
Thanks for all you do.

[signature]

THE
TRUE GEOGRAPHY
OF OUR COUNTRY

JEFFERSON'S
CARTOGRAPHIC
VISION

Joel Kovarsky

UNIVERSITY OF VIRGINIA PRESS

Charlottesville & London

University of Virginia Press

Printed in the United States of America on acid-free paper

First published 2014

9 8 7 6 5 4 3 2 1

Library of Congress Cataloging-in-Publication Data
Kovarsky, Joel.
    The true geography of our country : Jefferson's cartographic vision /
Joel Kovarsky.
        pages   cm
    Includes bibliographical references and index.
    ISBN 978-0-8139-3558-4 (cloth : alk. paper) — ISBN 978-0-8139-3559-1
(e-book)
    1. Jefferson, Thomas, 1743–1826—Knowledge—Geography. 2. United
States—Geography. 3. Geography—History—19th century. I. Title.
    E332.2.K68 2014
    973.4'6092—dc23
    [B]
                                                                    2013050489

For Deborah, Lee, and Ian

A great deal is yet wanting to ascertain the true
geography of our country; more indeed as to its
longitudes than latitudes. Towards this we have done
too little for ourselves and depended too long on the
ancient and inaccurate observations of other nations.
You are wiping off this reproach, and will, I hope, be long
continued in that work. All this will be for a future race
when the superlunary geography will have become the
object of my contemplations. Yet I do not wish it the less.
On the same principle on which I am still planting trees,
to yield their shade and ornament half a century hence.
— Thomas Jefferson to Andrew Ellicott, June 1812

CONTENTS

❈ ❈ ❈

❈ ❈

❈

ILLUSTRATIONS

❀ ❀ ❀
❀ ❀
❀

ACKNOWLEDGMENTS

❀ ❀ ❀
❀ ❀
❀

This book would never have taken shape without the continued encouragement of the retired director of the University of Virginia Press, Penelope J. Kaiserlian. Likewise, I am beholden to the ongoing copyediting assistance of my friend Joanne Foster and Mark Mones at the University of Virginia Press. I thank my wife, Deborah Kovarsky, for her patience, especially with our study floor piled high with books and papers for several years.

Chapter 6, "Foreshadowing Manifest Destiny," took shape during a short-term fellowship at the Robert H. Smith International Center for Jefferson Studies at Monticello. The Digital Curation Services of the University of Virginia Library provided ongoing assistance with the numerous images from the Albert and Shirley Small Special Collections Library. David Rumsey kindly gave permission to use multiple images from his renowned online map collection, and numerous other images were obtained from the map collections of the Library of Congress American Memory site. I am also grateful to numerous staff members at the University of Virginia Press for their guidance in preparation of the final manuscript.

A visitor walking into the expansive entrance hall at Jefferson's Monticello is immediately struck by the range of visual displays: the great clock; the busts of Alexander Hamilton, Michel-Étienne Turgot, and Voltaire; the paintings depicting John Adams, Amerigo Vespucci, and a young Native American chieftain; and numerous other artifacts native to North America. Along with these treasures, a remarkable and unique cartographic display is intended to impress and instruct, comprising wall maps of continental Africa, Asia, Europe, and North America (including the United States); a later variant of the Fry-Jefferson map of Virginia (coauthored by his father); a reduced version of Cruz-Cano's map of South America; and Bishop Madison's early-nineteenth-century map of Virginia.[1]

Literature about the enigmatic polymath Thomas Jefferson is voluminous and seemingly ever expanding. The genre is an industry unto itself, and the varied biographical tomes and papers include eulogies, deifications, vilifications, and combinations thereof. Almost every aspect of Jefferson's life has been discussed and dissected.

In these varied attempts to describe his multifaceted intellectual pursuits, numerous labels have been attached to Jefferson. He has been called agronomist, American sphinx, American synecdoche, architect, archaeologist, astronomer, author, botanist, ethnologist, linguist, paleontologist, philosopher, scientist, and more.[2] He has also, upon occasion, been described as a geographer.[3] Because he is only known to have produced a single printed map (fig. 1), his name is not usually included in the pantheon of major American mapmakers,[4] but this oversight seriously underestimates his interest in and use of cartographic materials, which is a focus of this book.

FIGURE I. *A Map of the Country between Albemarle Sound and Lake Erie, Comprehending the Whole of Virginia, Maryland, Delaware, and Pennsylvania,* by Thomas Jefferson, published by John Stockdale, London, 1787. This was Jefferson's only published, printed (engraved) map, although several other personal sketch maps appear in *Notes on the State of Virginia.* (Tracy W. McGregor Library of American History, Albert and Shirley Small Special Collections Library, University of Virginia)

The word "cartography" was not in use in Jefferson's time.[5] Still, there is little doubt that he studied maps throughout his long career as a lawyer and politician, and into his "twilight years" at Monticello.

It is not precisely known how Jefferson viewed the scope of geography, which was not a well-established academic subject during his time.[6] Nor is it my intent to characterize Jefferson as a professional geographer: he was not. Instead, I intend to demonstrate the importance of geography and maps as the foundational scaffolding for his varied lifelong pursuits in these pages. By Jefferson's time, the world had already seen the Age of Exploration and the great sea voyages of Captain James Cook, and during the eighteenth century geography could be considered the "mother of all sciences," because it preceded the rapid specializations of the mid- to late-nineteenth-century academic world.[7] Geographical knowledge was intellectually central—even if shrouded by ignorance—to the imperial interests of the expanding European and Asian nations of the Enlightenment.

It is possible to get some idea of Jefferson's views by looking at his various libraries, which over time contained more than fifty different dictionaries, as well as more than three hundred works pertaining to geography. One of those many dictionaries, often consulted today to gauge the use of the English language during the eighteenth century, was the fourth edition of Samuel Johnson's *A Dictionary of the English Language: in which the Words are deduced from their Originals, and Illustrated in their different Significations by Examples from the best Writers; To which are prefixed, a History of the Language, and an English Grammar,* published in 1775. And though Jefferson did not spare the lexicographer from criticisms of the work, he acknowledged the importance of the reference, noting that "he [Johnson] is however, on the whole, our best etymologist, unless we ascend a step higher to the Anglo-Saxon vocabulary; and he has set the good example of collating the English word with it's kindred word in the several Northern dialects."[8] Johnson defined geography thus:

> Geography, in the strict sense, signifies the knowledge of the circles of the earthly globe, and the situation of the various parts of earth. When it is taken in a little larger sense, it includes the knowledge of the seas also; and in the largest sense of all, it extends to the various customs, habits, and governments of nations.[9]

Jefferson's decades-long use of geographic and cartographic materials, including his own extensive writing and correspondence, clearly justifies the most expansive application of the definition.

Amateur and professional students of the history of the colonial era and the early republic are well aware that much of the subject focuses on land and landscape.[10] This is hardly surprising, given the imperial conflicts—largely Spanish, French, and British—that shaped the course of eighteenth- and nineteenth-century territorial expansions and the formative years of the United States. And yet, European ignorance of the western continental landscape defined that history as much as what was known.[11]

Jefferson's life and careers were immersed in that history, beginning with his childhood, when he learned about the land from his father, Peter Jefferson, and continuing past his presidential years. Geographical thought and map use were central to his presidency, best exemplified by his intense involvement with the planning for the expeditions of Meriwether Lewis and William Clark to the Pacific Northwest and William Dunbar and George Hunter to portions of the Louisiana Territory.[12] His role in both instances was particularly remarkable, given that Jefferson never ventured west of Staunton, Virginia, nestled on the western edge of the Shenandoah Valley.

Jefferson's reliance on maps was not entirely novel for his time, although his own level of knowledge of geographic and cartographic sources was certainly unusual. The use of maps for delineating property boundaries dates to antiquity,[13] and their historical role in boundary disputes between nations is well known.[14] Henry VIII had worried that lack of adequate cartographic information would put him at risk of Spanish invasion. Maps as way-finding devices were just beginning to enjoy increased use during Jefferson's time, and like so many other travelers of his era, he often relied on written itineraries for his journeys.[15]

The prominent placement of the large wall maps in the great entrance hall at Monticello exemplifies the importance of maps in Jefferson's thinking.[16] His map collection was not focused on the historical or monetary value of the object, as might be the case with many modern collectors. He was instead more interested in the accuracy and utility of then-current cartographic content, following his long-standing commitment to "useful knowledge," a pattern consistently reflected in the development of his "Great Library."[17]

That geography was an important component of Jefferson's upbringing and future pursuits is hardly astonishing, given the central role of the subject in the education and literacy of many landed gentry from the late seventeenth to the early nineteenth century in the North American colonies. Geographical texts were precursors to modern history texts and were discussed not only in the local schools but also around the family table. Colonial landowners generally possessed rudimentary land surveying skills.[18] And in contrast to some modern geographers, Jefferson's use of geography did not foster conflict between the utility of text and maps: he simultaneously used both textual and visual linguistic elements as practical, decision-making tools.[19]

Jefferson's best-known and only published book, *Notes on the State of Virginia* (1785), was an important regional and textual geographic and chorographic treatise, styled to some extent after other contemporary published geographies.[20] The book drew upon his personal journals about the varied features of his state, which were stemmed from his responses to twenty-two numbered queries that the French chargé d'affaires in North America, François Barbé-Marbois, sent to him in 1781.[21]

Jefferson's Great Library, which in 1814 became the foundation for the Library of Congress, was the result of nearly five decades of acquisitions.[22] Several hundred volumes pertaining to geography, and a few individual maps, are detailed in published lists of his collection.[23] These inventories do not reflect the scope of his personal map holdings, nor do they provide a measure of the maps available to him and those he actually used. Much as readers interested in Jefferson and cartography might wish for a complete listing of the maps he owned, the prospects are dim, as much of his Great Library was destroyed by fire, and his memorandum books, which document the purchase of individual maps and group of maps, almost never provide added item-specific detail.[24]

An understanding of Jefferson's use of maps and his professions about the importance of geographic and cartographic materials—not simply confined to his presidential tenure, but throughout his life—is best derived by examining his varied and extensive writings. Jefferson understood the importance of land measurement and was involved with the development of the United States Public Land Survey System and United States Coastal Survey.[25] And his farm and garden books speak volumes about his background in land surveying and geography.

Jefferson's extensive correspondence, estimated in the range of eighteen thousand letters, contains numerous examples of geographical commentary, as well as discussions of various cartographic and astronomical subjects. He communicated locally and internationally about maps and mapping, not only in the context of his planning and following the major expeditions launched during his presidency, but also through ongoing exchanges with the likes of Andrew Ellicott, Pierre L'Enfant, Bishop James Madison (President Madison's cousin), and Alexander von Humboldt. Among Jefferson's writings, letters and other documents, are various manuscript surveys of his landholdings and numerous architectural drawings portraying the early design of what he considered one of his most important achievements: the "Academical Village" of the University of Virginia. Many of these local representations are chorographic—that is, relating to the art of describing or mapping a region or district.

This book is divided into eight chapters. Chapter 1, "A Surveyor's House," details Jefferson's longtime interest in land surveying, including his involvement with the early Public Land Survey, the founding of the U.S. Coast Survey, the planning for the District of Columbia and the Virginia State Capitol, and the ongoing design and reworking both of his landmark home at Monticello and the University of Virginia. Chapter 2, "A Virginia Geography," discusses his *Notes on the State of Virginia* as a geographical work, while chapter 3, "Library of the Geography of America," considers the geographical holdings of his Great Library. Chapter 4, "Jefferson as Expedition Planner," focuses on his role in planning the journeys of Lewis and Clark, Dunbar and Hunter, and Freeman and Curtis. Chapter 5, "A Geography of Letters," addresses his extensive exchange of letters—dealing with a wide range of geographic and cartographic subjects—with numerous individuals over many decades, and chapter 6, "Foreshadowing Manifest Destiny," uses Jefferson as a lens for the geographic and cartographic foreshadowing of the nation's continental aspirations. Chapter 7, "Geographical Miscellanies," documents a range of Jefferson's geographically and cartographically related interests, including astronomy and meteorology. Finally, an epilogue attempts some synthesis of the various threads woven throughout the previous chapters.

Though others might have used a purely chronological approach, I feel that the clearest way to present and summarize Jefferson's long-standing and widespread reliance on and use of geographic and cartographic knowledge is through this topical format. A thematic approach allows the general reader to digest the diverse elements in a series of shorter, interrelated essays. Those specialized bits are, to the extent possible, organized chronologically.

The resulting work reflects substantial use of primary source documents such as maps and letters, enriched by extensive reliance on numerous secondary sources from the ever-expanding literature on Jeffersoniana. Quotations used in the text are left exactly as printed in the major cited transcriptions, with no attempt made to update spelling or syntax to conform to modern conventions. Many of these excerpts are drawn from Rotunda, the digital imprint of the University of Virginia Press. A non-subscription version of their American Founding Era Collection, which includes Jefferson's papers, is accessible via the open-access National Archives project "Founders Online," at http://founders.archives.gov/.

Many of the passages drawn from Jefferson's writings included herein are lengthy and intended to emphasize the critical roles of geography and maps as foundational elements of his intellectual processes, through progressive stages of his varied careers. These geographic and cartographic thoughts were central to Jefferson's enduring connection to the history of the continental expansion of the early American republic.

A SURVEYOR'S HOUSE

❀ ❀ ❀
❀ ❀
❀

The story of colonial America and the early republic is one of geography and empire, land and landscape, and control and measurement.[1] This geographical focus fostered the importance and popularity of training in the arts of surveying, which was one of the most common forms of vocational study in eighteenth-century North America.[2] The intense emphasis on the parceling of land in colonial Virginia derived directly from British customs and ongoing interests in the region.[3]

The landed gentry and their sons could not rely on ready availability of skilled professional help, prompting their need for some familiarity with existing surveying methods. This was the world into which Thomas Jefferson was born, and it is no surprise that some historians emphasize the importance of early instruction at his father's side, walking through the woods of the family lands, as a fledgling step toward his future interests.[4]

One reason for the accentuation of such training in colonial America was the revocation of New England land charters by the English Parliament in 1690. The resulting flurry of surveying has been characterized as a new and popular form of learning, joining descriptive writing to technical measurement. The field books surveyors produced were textual ledgers, and in many respects they were more important than the measurements themselves.[5]

Professionally trained surveyors were in short supply in the American colonies during the seventeenth and early eighteenth centuries. The needs of local landowners created an imperative demand for self-instruction, and resulted in a proliferation of printed guides. Contemporary newspapers carried advertisements for surveying instruction, and the number of handbooks—by necessity English imports—correspondingly increased.[6]

An appointment to the post of county surveyor was a path to social, political, and economic success. Virtually every surveyor of western lands in the colonies held the position of magistrate of the county court, including Peter Jefferson, Joshua Fry, George Carrington, John Donelson, Peter Fontaine, William Preston, and William Cabell II. Surveyors held numerous seats in the Virginia legislature, as well as lesser executive positions. By Thomas Jefferson's time, most of Virginia's land had been surveyed, so the enterprise was no longer a consistently profitable career. Nonetheless, the children of the last major generation of colonial surveyors were able to capitalize on the political connections of their families, and four nineteenth-century Virginia governors came from their ranks.[7]

It is easy to believe that young Thomas would have received ongoing instruction on operating and maintaining the family lands. He eventually inherited his father's surveying tools and a number of books related to travel and geography.[8] But these considerations might overstate the force of intellectual impact during his early years. Many of Thomas's contemporaries received similar instruction, yet very few of them developed the combination of intense intellectual and political involvements with land and landscape that characterized Jefferson from the early years of his legal practice. So many of his activities relied on knowledge of surveying principles: his frequent litigation of land claims, his long-standing development of the Monticello estate, the planning of the Virginia capitol building in Richmond, the decades of intense involvement in the design of the young nation's capital city in the District of Columbia, the inception of the U.S. Public Land Survey during his tenure with the Continental Congress, the planning of expeditions to the Pacific Northwest and within the Louisiana Territory during his presidency, and finally the surveying for and design of the Academical Village of the University of Virginia.

Thomas's great-grandfather, who was also named Thomas, was a seventeenth-century surveyor of roads for Henrico County, Virginia.[9] His father, Peter Jefferson, was eventually appointed surveyor for Albemarle County after being assistant surveyor to both William Mayo and Joshua Fry. Peter is best known for his coauthorship, with Fry, of the seminal *Map of the Inhabited Part of Virginia containing the whole Province of Maryland with part of Pensilvania, New Jersey and North Carolina.*[10] From October 1773 until April 1774, Thomas officially held the post of Albemarle County surveyor, at a time when he was questioning an ongoing commitment to his legal career. (There is no evidence indicated that he was actively engaged in surveying or that he signed a single survey during that appointment.[11])

That brief and purely titular stint as county surveyor does not accurately reflect Jefferson's exposure to, interest in, and use of surveying principles during his life. His formal education at the Latin School under the tutelage of the Reverend James Maury and at the College of William and Mary under the guidance of William Small included instruction in elements of surveying, navigation, and fortification. At the time of Jefferson's attendance, the academic standards of the College of William and Mary were not of the caliber of the major institutions of England and Scotland. Still, his education in surveying and related areas was unquestionably guided and fostered by Small, who served as professor of natural philosophy.[12]

William and Mary did not specifically train surveyors, and the quality of colonial practitioners did not match those in the British Isles. It is not clear why Jefferson was chosen for his short and apparently uneventful stint as Albemarle County surveyor, although it is probable that the fact he was considered a young gentleman of some social—and economic—standing was a significant factor, as a portion of the surveying fees were paid to the college.[13] He apparently made some attempt to prepare for the position, having acquired an array of related scientific tools, including Marshall's Meridian Instrument.[14]

Those years of exposure to the practical side of surveying, from childhood through his stint as Albemarle County surveyor, would influence Jefferson throughout his professional careers and personal life. He understood the value of astronomical observations for accurately surveying the land, which resulted in his lifelong interests in astronomy and his plans to include the science in basic educational programs at college and university levels. This emphasis was not directed toward the primary study of celestial bodies, but rather on more accurate measurement of the land,[15] a reflection of his interest in "useful knowledge."[16]

Because so much of Jefferson's short legal career (1767–74) was occupied with land-claim disputes, a basic knowledge of the surveying process was essential to his profession. Nearly half of Jefferson's cases involved land claims or boundary disputes, and many of these filings

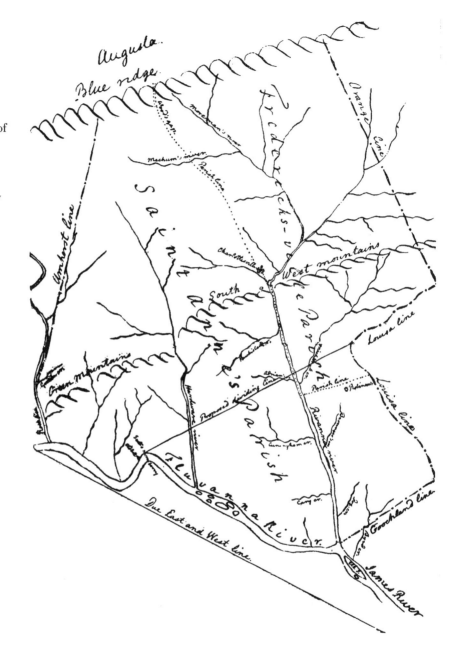

were necessarily accompanied by land surveys.[17] Those surveys were not prepared by Jefferson himself, but the ongoing evaluation process facilitated his understanding of the importance of land measurement for the placement of boundaries, experience that bore direct relevance for his future political career.

The earliest map Jefferson is known to have drawn, produced in 1777, was related to a proposal to create Fluvanna County from the existing lands of Albemarle County. After Jefferson surveyed the land, he produced a map indicating the proposed line of division (fig. 2).[18] On 31 March 1781, as governor of Virginia, Jefferson appointed the Reverends James Madison and Robert Andrews to help survey the boundary extension between Virginia and Pennsylvania:

> The principles on which the Boundary between Pensylvania and this State is to be run having been fixed it is now proposed by President Reid that Commissioners proceed to execute the work from the Termination of Masons and Dixons Line to the Completion of the five Degrees of Longitude and thence on a meridian to the Ohio.
>
> We propose that the extent of the five Degrees of longitude shall be determined by celestial Observations. Of Course it will require one set of Astronomers to be at Philadelphia and another at Fort Pitt.[19]

In such matters as these, Jefferson was well equipped to pursue his surveying interests. He owned several surveyors' compasses, also called "circumferentors," which were used to measure horizontal angles. Sometime after 1786, he produced a list of his "Mathematical Apparatus," which included several telescopes, an equatorial, and a theodolite, the latter two designed by Jesse Ramsden, a Yorkshireman renowned for the production of scientific instruments. (The theodolite eventually superseded the circumferentor.) He also listed a Gunter's (surveyor's) chain, a Hadley's circle of Borda, a pocket sextant, a perambulator (surveyor's wheel), and Marshall's meridian instrument.[20] Jefferson had obtained the Universal Equatorial Instrument (theodolite) previously owned by a prominent military engineer and cartographer, John William Gerard de Brahm, which was likely the only one of its kind in the United States at the time, and modified the instrument by adding a twelve-inch telescope (fig. 3).[21] As part of his fascination with distance

FIGURE 3.
Several of Jefferson's surveying
instruments, *from top to bottom*:
Ramsden theodolite, surveying
compass (not Jefferson's, but he
almost certainly had one), and
pedestal telescope. (Thomas
Jefferson Foundation at Monticello,
photographs by Edward Owen)

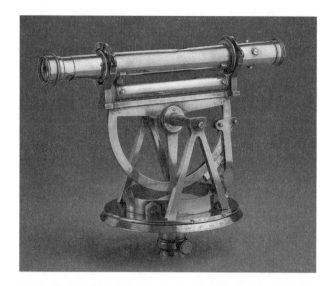

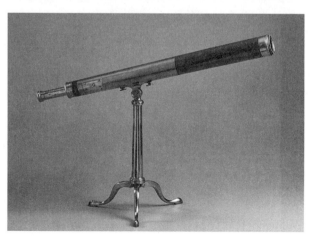

measurement, Jefferson possessed a number of odometers, and he even tried, unsuccessfully, to produce his own.[22]

UNITED STATES PUBLIC LAND (AMERICAN RECTANGULAR) SURVEY

One of Jefferson's most important projects involving the issues of land surveying began in 1780, while he was governor of Virginia. He was integrally involved in the process of ceding certain western Virginia lands to foster the expansion of the evolving confederation of states. On 2 January 1781, the Virginia legislature ceded nearly all its claims to land north of the Ohio River to the U.S. government. This cession was accepted in October of 1783.[23] In a committee report dated 30 April 1784, just prior to his appointment as commissioner to France, Jefferson carefully described both the method by which these lands would be divided into a rectangular grid, and the intent to establish a public land office:

> Be it ordained by the United States in Congress assembled, that the territory ceded by individual States to the United States, when the same shall have been purchased of the Indian inhabitants, & laid off into States, shall be disposed of in the following manner. It shall be divided into Hundreds of ten geographical miles square, each mile containing 6086 feet and four tenths of a foot, by lines to be run & marked due North & South, & others crossing these at right angles, the first of which lines, each way, shall be at ten miles distance from one of the corner [i.e., establishing a rectangular grid] . . .
>
> For laying off the said territory, Surveyors shall be appointed . . . to divide the same into hundreds, by lines in the directions, & at the intervals before mentioned, which lines shall be measured with a chain, shall be plainly marked by Chops, or marks on the trees & shall be exactly described on a plat, whereon shall be noted at their proper distances, all watercourses, mountains & other remarkeable & permanent things over or near which such lines shall pass.
>
> The Hundreds being laid off and marked . . . shall then proceed to divide each Hundred of his district into lots as before directed . . . and measuring, marking & platting the said dividing

lines thereof in the manner before directed for the Hundreds, save only that the lines of the lots shall be distinguished by a single mark on each tree, and those of the hundreds by three marks . . . The surveyors shall pay due & constant attention to the variation of the magnetic meridian, & shall run & note all lines by the true meridian, certifying with every plat what was the variation at the time of running the lines thereon noted.[24]

Several late-eighteenth-century land ordinances were enacted by the U.S. Congress to establish procedures for settlement and incorporation of the Northwest Territory, and the Land Ordinance of 1785 super-seded the Land Ordinance of 1784. In a letter to David Hartley dated 5 September 1785, Jefferson wrote:

Congress have lately purchased the Indian right to nearly the whole of the land lying in the new state bounded by lake Erie, Pennsylvania and the Ohio. The Northwestern corner alone is reserved to the Delawares and Wiandots. I expect a purchase is also concluded with other tribes for a considerable proportion of the state next to this on the North side of the Ohio. They have passed an ordinance establishing a land office. . . .

I think it probable that Vermont will be made independent . . . Le Maine will probably in time be also permitted to separate from Massachusetts. . . . Whenever the people of Kentuckey shall have agreed among themselves, my friends write me word that Virginia will consent to their separation. They will constitute the new state on the South side of Ohio, joining Virginia. North-Carolina, by an act of their assembly, ceded to Congress all their lands Westward of the Alleghaney.[25]

In early November of 1791, at the request of President Washington, Jefferson, as secretary of state, prepared his "Report on the Public Lands," which discussed future resolution of southwestern boundary disputes with Spain, allowing for the westward expansion of the republic. During the preparation of this report, Jefferson not only conducted his own extensive research, but also consulted a number of other officials: William Blount, governor of the southwest territory; Alexander Martin, governor of North Carolina; Arthur St. Clair, governor of the

Northwest Territory; Trent Coxe, assistant secretary of the treasury; and John Harvie, head of the Virginia Land Office.[26]

Following the inception of the U.S. Public Land Survey System,[27] Jefferson decided that the nation's capital should have its own meridian, thereby facilitating the production of accurate maps to document the nation's territorial expansion. He felt, as did many of his contemporaries, that mapping the growth of the United States should not rely on practices in England or any other foreign nation. In 1791, while serving as secretary of state, he directed Andrew Ellicott, one of the most skilled surveyors in the country, to map the Territory of Columbia. Jefferson proposed a new meridian to run through the center of the Capitol building as the starting point for a future layout of streets in the federal city. In 1804 he instructed the surveyor general of the Mississippi Territory, Isaac Briggs, to create a north–south line at the president's house. Assisting Briggs was the recently appointed surveyor of the District of Columbia, Nicholas King. Despite this groundwork, development of a national prime meridian stalled for more than forty years.[28]

Jefferson also saw the need for a national surveyor. In 1801, the first year of his presidency, he proposed creation of the post of surveyor general of the United States and, without additional congressional consultation, offered Andrew Ellicott the position. Ellicott declined, for a number of reasons, and in 1803 Jefferson turned to Jared Mansfield, a talented mathematician who had been a soldier and teacher at West Point, who accepted the position.[29]

Jefferson also understood the military and commercial importance of surveying the young nation's coasts. During the final year of his presidency, he convinced Congress to authorize funding for the creation of the U.S. Coast Survey. He signed into law "An act to provide for surveying coasts of the United States" on 10 February 1807. Jefferson collaborated with his secretary of the treasury, Albert Gallatin, in planning the project, and considered numerous candidates (all known to Jefferson) to head the survey. Eventually the two agreed on Ferdinand Rudolph Hassler as the man for the job.[30] But due to a number of organizational problems, including difficulties obtaining the desired scientific equipment, the work of the Coast Survey did not begin for nearly a decade after Jefferson's presidency had ended.[31]

For two and a half decades, from his days as a member of the Continental Congress in 1783 and extending through his presidency, Jefferson was involved with nearly every aspect of the site selection, development plan, and construction of the evolving city of Washington, D.C. This required not only a working knowledge of surveying, but also of topographical considerations pertaining to site selection and architectural design skills involving perspective and scale—considerations that overlapped with his ongoing development of Monticello and his future role in the development of the University of Virginia. Jefferson has been called a "city planner" in a time before that modern form of specialization was formally recognized. This label is, for some, a bit ironic, given the known anti-urban stance of some of his political discourse.[32] The federal city was the first attempt to build a national capital city under supervision of a government in the form of a representational democracy,[33] and thus was a novel and daunting undertaking.[34]

The eventual location of the new federal city evolved over a decade. During the Pennsylvania (Philadelphia) Mutiny of 1783, a group of armed soldiers protesting delinquent back pay for services in the Continental Army caused a fearful Congress to evacuate Philadelphia. Congress had to consider a new and hopefully permanent location for a seat of government. In 1790, Jefferson, James Madison, and Alexander Hamilton brokered a compromise giving President George Washington the authority to select a site along the Potomac River:

> BE it enacted by the Senate and House of Representatives of the United States of America in Congress assembled, That a district of territory, not exceeding ten miles square, to be located as hereafter directed on the river Potomack, at some place between the mouths of the Eastern-Branch and Connogochegue be, and the same is hereby accepted for the permanent seat of the government of the United States.[35]

In early 1791, at the behest of President Washington, Jefferson arranged for Major Andrew Ellicott to begin surveying the area planned for the new capital. Shortly thereafter, Jefferson requested Major Pierre Charles L'Enfant to proceed to George town where you will find Mr. Ellicot employed in making a survey and map of the federal territory. The special object of asking your aid is to have drawings of the particular grounds most likely to be approved for the site of the federal town and buildings. You will therefore be pleased to begin on the Eastern branch, and proceed from thence upwards, laying down the hills, vallies, morasses, and waters between that, the Patowmac, the Tyber, and the road leading from George town to the Eastern branch, and connecting the whole with certain fixed points of the map Mr. Ellicot is preparing. Some idea of the height of the hills above the base on which they stand would be desireable.[36]

On 17 March 1791 Jefferson again wrote to L'Enfant:

Your favor of the 11. inst. has been duly recieved. Between the date of that and your reciept of the present, it is probable that the most important parts of the ground towards the Eastern branch will have been delineated. However, whether they are or not, as the President will go on within two or three days, and would wish to have under his eye, when at Georgetown, a drawing also of the principal lineaments of the ground between Rock creek and the Tyber, you are desired, immediately on the reciept of this, to commence the survey of that part, beginning at the river, and proceeding towards the parts back of that till his arrival. If the meanders of these two creeks and of the river between them should not have been already laid down either by yourself or Mr. Ellicot, it is desired that Mr. Ellicot should immediately do this while you shall be employed on the interior ground, in order that the work may be as much advanced as possible on the arrival of the President, and that you will be so good as to notify this to Mr. Ellicot.[37]

L'Enfant then asked Jefferson for help in obtaining "grand city" plans, to which Jefferson responded:

I am favored with your letter of the 4th. inst. and in compliance with your request I have examined my papers and found the plans of Frankfort on the Mayne, Carlsruhe, Amsterdam Strasburg, Paris, Orleans, Bordeaux, Lyons, Montpelier, Marseilles, Turin and Milan, which I send in a roll by this post. They are on large and accurate scales, having been procured by me while in those respective cities myself. As they are connected with the notes I made in my travels, and often necessary to explain them to myself, I will beg your care of them and to return them when no longer useful to you.[38]

It can be argued that Jefferson and L'Enfant deserve nearly equal credit for the early plan of Washington, D.C. (fig. 4). After inevitable conflicts with Jefferson and others, L'Enfant was dismissed from his position in February of 1792:

> From your letter . . . and declarations . . . it is understood that you absolutely decline acting under the authority of the present Commissioners . . . I am instructed by the President to inform you that notwithstanding the desire he has entertained to preserve your agency in the business the condition upon which it is to be done is inadmissible, & your services must be at an end.[39]

Andrew Ellicott was then handed the task of adapting the existing plan from paper to the actual site. As a result, he prepared a more detailed and accurate version without altering the basic design (fig. 5).[40]

During his first presidential term, Jefferson was involved with nearly every aspect of implementing the plans for the federal city. In August of 1802 he appointed Nicholas King surveyor for the city, and in 1803 he appointed Benjamin Henry Latrobe surveyor of public buildings. When Jefferson left the presidency is 1809, supervision of the ongoing capital project fell to Latrobe.[41]

MONTICELLO AND THE ACADEMICAL VILLAGE

A number of published works highlight Jefferson's pioneering work as an architect, designing buildings and landscapes. Although he never relied on his architectural skills to earn a living, both the decades-long planning and building of Monticello and his commitment to the establishment of the Academical Village of the University of Virginia are testaments to his extensive skills in various elements of architectural design and execution.[42] Jefferson's knowledge of surveying and geography were at the heart of his architectural accomplishments, and his understanding of the importance of scale was crucial. The intellectual links between cartography and architectural design are longstanding.

Both relate to conceptualization of physical space, draw upon the principles of scale and perspective, involve mathematical modeling,[43] and require some knowledge of surveying and topographical analysis.

By 1770, Jefferson had already invested significant time and thought concerning Monticello's future design. In his 21 February letter to John Page, shortly after his Shadwell plantation house had been destroyed by fire, he wrote: "If this conflagration, by which I am burned out of a home, had come before I had advanced so far in preparing another, I do not know but I might have cherished some treasonable thoughts of leaving these my native hills."[44] In late 1771, Jefferson set down elaborate plans for the development of Monticello's grounds in his account book.[45]

Over the years, Jefferson sketched numerous, evolving plans for Monticello's grounds (figs. 6 and 7). As with the designation "city planner," the formal title of "landscape planner" did not exist in the mid-eighteenth century. Nonetheless, Jefferson qualified as such for his work at Monticello and the University of Virginia. His combined knowledge of surveying, architecture, local geography and meteorology, and local plant life were likely second to none among his contemporaries.[46] Jefferson's garden and farm books each provide additional evidence of his background in and dependence on his knowledge of surveying and geography for his ongoing projects at Monticello.[47] This is not to say that his early architectural drawings, grounds surveys, or land surveys were sophisticated relative to European counterparts—they were not. But he was quite adept by contemporary North American standards, and his mechanical drawing skills were well established.[48]

Planning, selecting the Charlottesville site, and supervising the building of the University of Virginia was, by any measure, the capstone of Jefferson's life. Although the project was not officially authorized until 1817, when Jefferson was seventy-four years old, he had been contemplating it for nearly a decade. In a letter dated 6 May 1810, he commented on the construction of colleges to the trustees for the lottery of East Tennessee College:

> I consider the common plan followed in this country, but not in others, of making one large and expensive building, as unfortunately erroneous. It is infinitely better to erect a small and separate lodge for each professorship, with only a hall below for

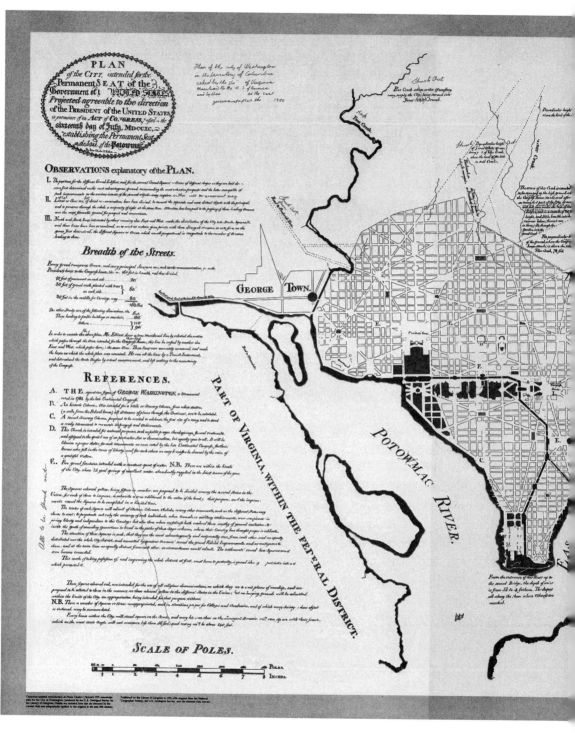

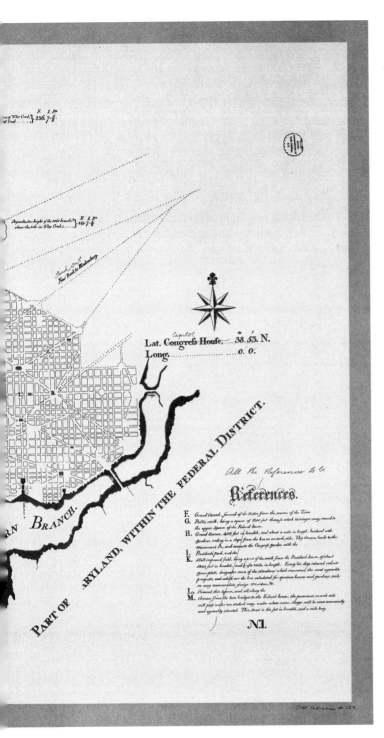

FIGURE 4.

Plan of the city intended for the permanent seat of the government of t[he] United States: projected agreeable to the direction of the President of the United States, in pursuance of an act of Congress, passed on the sixteenth day of July, MDCCXC, "establishing the permanent seat on the bank of the Potowmac," by Pierre Charles L'Enfant, originally drawn in 1791. The version shown here is a computer-assisted reproduction, published by the Library of Congress in 1991 with support from the National Geographic Society, the U.S. Geological Survey, and the National Park Service. (American Memory Collection, Library of Congress)

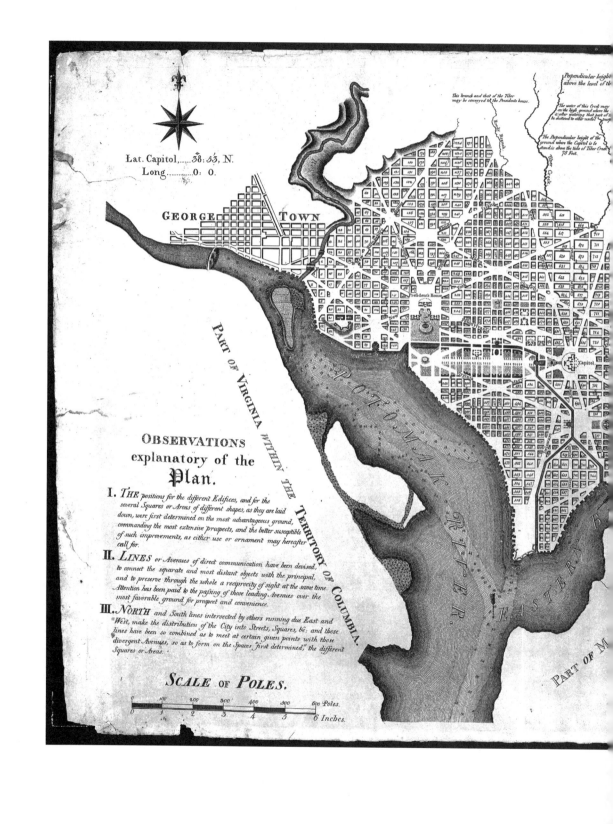

Lat. Capitol,....38:53, N.
Long..........0: 0.

GEORGE TOWN

PART OF VIRGINIA WITHIN THE TERRITORY OF COLUMBIA.

President's House

Capitol

POTOMAK RIVER

EASTERN B.

PART OF M

This branch and that of the Tiber
may be conveyed to the President's house.

Perpendicular height
above the level of th

The water of this Creek may
on the high ground where the
either watering that part of th
be destined to either useful pur

The Perpendicular height of the
ground where the Capitol is to
stand is above the tide of Tiber Creek
78 Feet.

Rock Branch

Tiber Creek

OBSERVATIONS
explanatory of the
Plan.

I. *THE* positions for the different Edifices, and for the
several Squares or Areas of different shapes, as they are laid
down, were first determined on the most advantageous ground,
commanding the most extensive prospects, and the better susceptible
of such improvements, as either use or ornament may hereafter
call for.

II. *LINES* or Avenues of direct communication have been devised,
to connect the separate and most distant objects with the principal,
and to preserve through the whole a reciprocity of sight at the same time.
Attention has been paid to the passing of those leading Avenues over the
most favorable ground for prospect and convenience.

III. *NORTH* and South lines intersected by others running due East and
West, make the distribution of the City into Streets, Squares, &c; and those
lines have been so combined as to meet at certain given points with those
divergent Avenues, so as to form on the Spaces "first determined," the different
Squares or Areas.

SCALE OF POLES.

100   200   300   400   500   600 Poles.
0   1   2   3   4   5   6 Inches.

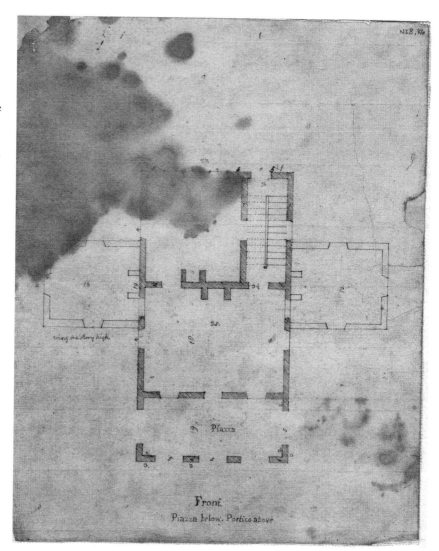

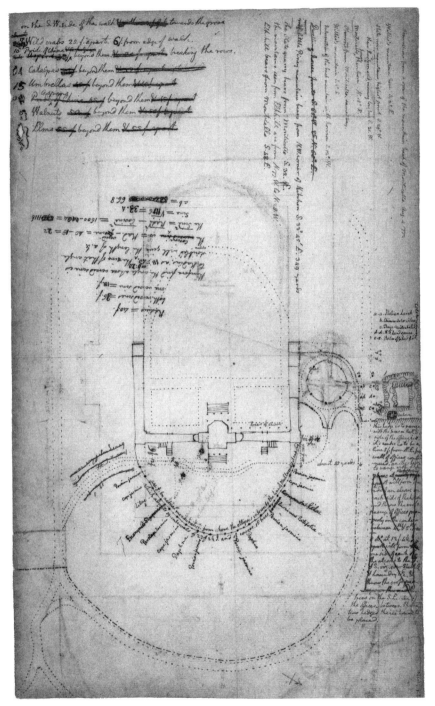

FIGURE 7.
Monticello: mountaintop layout (plan). Drawing by Thomas Jefferson, before May 1768. (Coolidge Collection of Thomas Jefferson Manuscripts, N61/K34, Massachusetts Historical Society)

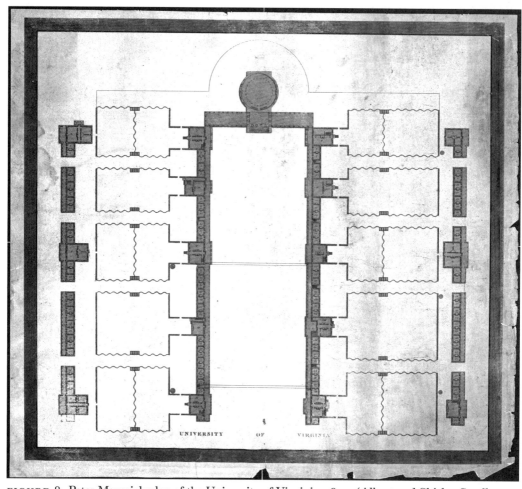

UNIVERSITY OF VIRGINIA

FIGURE 8. Peter Maverick plan of the University of Virginia, 1825. (Albert and Shirley Small Special Collections Library, accession #6552/6552-a, University of Virginia)

his class and two chambers above for himself; joining these lodges by barracks for a certain portion of the students, opening into a covered way to give a dry communication between all the schools. The whole of these arranged around an open square of grass and trees would make it what it should be in fact, an academical village . . . These separate buildings, too, might be erected successively and occasionally, as the number of professorships and students should be increased.[49]

Jefferson also sought outside advice from William Thornton and Benjamin Latrobe, although the remarkable architectural conceptualization of the university as a whole was Jefferson's creation. The separate library building and housing of departments, along with the general grand scope of the plan, had never been seen in any American university, and the particular combination of elements was arguably unique in the larger world as well.[50] Most of Jefferson's extant sketch plans for the grounds (fig. 8) are held by either the University of Virginia or the Massachusetts Historical Society.[51] All support the assertion that Jefferson's knowledge of local geographies and surveying suffused his architectural works.

That Jefferson's abilities in architecture and urban planning influenced and were influenced by his knowledge of geography and mapping is undeniable. His knowledge and ongoing experience in the planning of the District of Columbia and his monumental work in the creation and ongoing design of the University of Virginia were outgrowths of his geographic and cartographic skills and interests.

A VIRGINIA GEOGRAPHY

❋ ❋ ❋
❋ ❋
❋

Jefferson's *Notes on the State of Virginia,* like much of his writing and political thinking, has been both criticized and praised.[1] It has been by turns denigrated and lauded as perhaps the most important scientific and political book written by a native U.S. citizen before 1785.[2] This work, a subject of discussion in nearly every major biography of Jefferson,[3] is also a regional geographical treatise, one of the earliest published pertaining to a portion of the fledgling nation by an American author. It is certainly the earliest major textual chorography, written by one of its most prominent citizens, of the early republic.[4] And though the *Notes* contains Jefferson's only published printed map, it is a mistake to use that map as a main focus for a general discussion of the work.

Jedidiah Morse, father of the inventor of Morse code, is usually given titular pride of place as the father of American geography. However, the initial French edition of Jefferson's work appeared in 1785, followed by the English edition in 1787.[5] The text of Morse's Virginia entry through several editions of his *American Geography; or, A View of the Present Situation of the United States of America* copied Jefferson nearly word for word, and Morse clearly cites Jefferson as the main source of his information.[6]

Jefferson's *Notes* came into being through the formal queries that François Marbois, the future Marquis de Barbé-Marbois, distributed in the fall of 1780 to various congressional leaders from the original thirteen colonies. Marbois's questions stemmed from the French government's desire to gather information about the nascent nation. Although Jefferson's was not the only response to the list, his was by far the most detailed and thoughtful. This was no accident; he had long been in the habit of making personal notations of diverse details he deemed relevant to the state of Virginia.

For the published version of his *Notes,* Jefferson developed twenty-three queries.[7] At least fifteen of these focused on topics of geographical significance: boundaries of Virginia; rivers; sea ports; mountains; cascades; productions mineral, vegetable, and animal; climate; population; aborigines; counties and towns; colleges, buildings, and roads; religion; manners; manufactures; and subjects of commerce (fig. 9). Though Jefferson revised his responses over the years, there is no surviving record of his original answers to the Marbois queries.[8] Even after publication of the English edition of the *Notes,* Jefferson continued to annotate his own copy with new material, with an eye to future revisions.[9]

Although geography was considered a necessary part of a "gentleman's" education, it did not develop in England or the United States as a formal, independent academic discipline until the mid-nineteenth century. The notion of geographic subject matter—as a mathematical construct based on latitude and longitude and a textual/descriptive tradition—had already been established.[10] Although Jefferson's writings displayed elements of both components, the descriptive tradition is clearly more evident.

Query I supplies a discussion of Virginia's boundaries, setting a geographic and cartographic tone, supplying longitudinal and latitudinal measurements, and discussing their origins:

Virginia is bounded on the East by the Atlantic: on the North by a line of latitude, crossing the Eastern Shore through Watkins's Point, being about 37°.57′ North latitude; from thence by a streight line to Cinquac, near the mouth of Patowmac; thence by the Patowmac, which is common to Virginia and Maryland, to the first fountain of its northern branch; thence by a meridian line, passing through that fountain till it intersects a line running East and West, in latitude 39°.43′.42.4″ which divides Maryland from Pennsylvania, and which was marked by Messrs. Mason and Dixon; thence by that line, and a continuation of it westwardly to the completion of five degrees of longitude from the eastern boundary of Pennsylvania, in the same latitude, and thence by a meridian line to the Ohio: On the West by the Ohio and Missisipi, to latitude 36°.30′. North: and on the South by the line of latitude last-mentioned. By admeasurements through nearly the whole of

FIGURE 9.
Contents page from
Jefferson's copy
of *Notes on the
State of Virginia,*
published by John
Stockdale, London,
1787. (Tracy W.
McGregor Library
of American History,
Albert and Shirley
Small Special
Collections Library,
University of
Virginia)

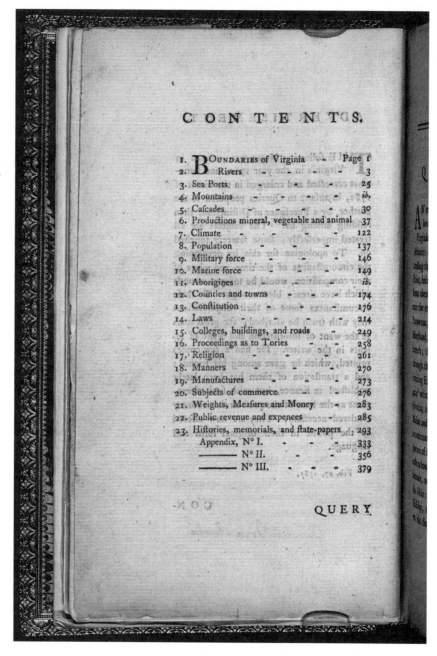

CONTENTS.

QUERY

this last line, and supplying the unmeasured parts from good data, the Atlantic and Missisipi, are found in this latitude to be 758 miles distant, equal to 13°.38′. of longitude, reckoning 55 miles and 3144 feet to the degree. This being our comprehension of longitude, that of our latitude, taken between this and Mason and Dixon's line, is 3°.13′.42.4″ equal to 223.3 miles, supposing a degree of a great circle to be 69 m. 864 f. as computed by Cassini. These boundaries include an area somewhat triangular, of 121525 square miles, whereof 79650 lie westward of the Allegany mountains, and 57034 westward of the meridian of the mouth of the Great Kanhaway. This state is therefore one third larger than the islands of Great Britain and Ireland, which are reckoned at 88357 square miles.

These limits result from, 1. The antient charters from the crown of England. 2. The grant of Maryland to the Lord Baltimore, and the subsequent determinations of the British court as to the extent of that grant. 3. The grant of Pennsylvania to William Penn, and a compact between the general assemblies of the commonwealths of Virginia and Pennsylvania as to the extent of that grant. 4. The grant of Carolina, and actual location of its northern boundary, by consent of both parties. 5. The treaty of Paris of 1763. 6. The confirmation of the charters of the neighbouring states by the convention of Virginia at the time of constituting their commonwealth. 7. The cession made by Virginia to Congress of all the lands to which they had title on the North side of the Ohio.[11]

Query II is a "notice of its rivers, rivulets, and how far they are navigable?" Emphasizing the importance of cartography, Jefferson writes, "An inspection of a map of Virginia, will give a better idea of the geography of its rivers, than any description in writing. Their navigation may be imperfectly noted." He then goes on to describe the state's major rivers,[12] demonstrating that he clearly understood the commercial and military importance of these waterways.

Query III, devoted to a "notice of the best sea-ports of the state, and how big are the vessels they can receive?" is quite short, simply stating that the only ports were small ones on rivers and creeks, and that any added discussion was to be found under Query II.[13]

Query IV, on mountains, begins with reference to the landmark map by Joshua Fry and Jefferson's father, Peter, and Lewis Evans's map of the middle British colonies:

> For the particular geography of our mountains I must refer to Fry and Jefferson's map of Virginia; and to Evans's analysis of his map of America for a more philosophical view of them than is to be found in any other work. It is worthy notice, that our mountains are not solitary and scattered confusedly over the face of the country; but that they commence at about 150 miles from the sea-coast, are disposed in ridges one behind another, running nearly parallel with the sea-coast, though rather approaching it as they advance north-eastwardly. To the south-west, as the tract of country between the sea-coast and the Mississipi becomes narrower, the mountains converge into a single ridge, which, as it approaches the Gulph of Mexico, subsides into plain country, and gives rise to some of the waters of that Gulph, and particularly to a river called the Apalachicola, probably from the Apalachies, an Indian nation formerly residing on it. Hence the mountains giving rise to that river, and seen from its various parts, were called the Apalachian mountains, being in fact the end or termination only of the great ridges passing through the continent. European geographers however extended the name northwardly as far as the mountains extended; some giving it, after their separation into different ridges, to the Blue ridge, others to the North mountain, others to the Alleghaney, others to the Laurel ridge, as may be seen in their different maps. But the fact I believe is, that none of these ridges were ever known by that name to the inhabitants, either native or emigrant, but as they saw them so called in European maps. In the same direction generally are the veins of lime-stone, coal and other minerals hitherto discovered: and so range the falls of our great rivers. But the courses of the great rivers are at right angles with these. James and Patowmac penetrate through all the ridges of mountains eastward of the Alleghaney.[14]

Query V, on cascades, notes:

> The only remarkable Cascade in this country, is that of the Falling Spring in Augusta. It is a water of James river, where it is called Jackson's river, rising in the warm spring mountains about

twenty miles South West of the warm spring, and flowing into that valley. About three quarters of a mile from its source, it falls over a rock 200 feet into the valley below. The sheet of water is broken in its breadth by the rock in two or three places, but not at all in its height. Between the sheet and rock, at the bottom, you may walk across dry. This Cataract will bear no comparison with that of Niagara, as to the quantity of water composing it; the sheet being only 12 or 15 feet wide above, and somewhat more spread below; but it is half as high again, the latter being only 156 feet, according to the mensuration made by order of M. Vaudreuil, Governor of Canada, and 130 according to a more recent account.[15]

Jefferson then goes on to describe the region's known caverns (Madison's Cave and Blowing Cave), and the Natural Bridge, which he calls the "most sublime of Nature's works." Included in this section is a sketch entitled "An Eye Draught of Madison's Cave," (fig. 10), which is arguably the first example of an American cave map.[16]

Query VI, entitled "productions mineral, vegetable and animal," is the longest in the book. It is intended as a "notice of the mines and other subterraneous riches; its trees, plants, fruits, &c." Mineral resources and their locations described include gold, lead, copper, black lead (graphite), pit coal, precious stones (amethyst being the most common), marble, limestone, various types of stone, types of earth, nitre, and salt. Various springs, medicinal and otherwise, are discussed. There is a tabular representation entitled "A comparative View of the Quadrupeds of Europe and of America," and a table of "Birds of Virginia." It is within this section that Jefferson devotes great effort to refute the infuriating claims of Georges-Louis Leclerc, Comte de Buffon, the French naturalist who had pointedly considered the climate and flora and fauna of the Americas inferior to those of Europe.[17]

Query VII relates to climate, and Jefferson writes:

Under the latitude of this query, I will presume it not improper nor unacceptable to furnish some data for estimating the climate of Virginia. Journals of observations on the quantity of rain, and degree of heat, being lengthy, confused, and too minute to produce general and distinct ideas, I have taken five years observations, to wit, from 1772 to 1777, made in Williamsburgh and its neighbourhood, have reduced them to an average for every month in the

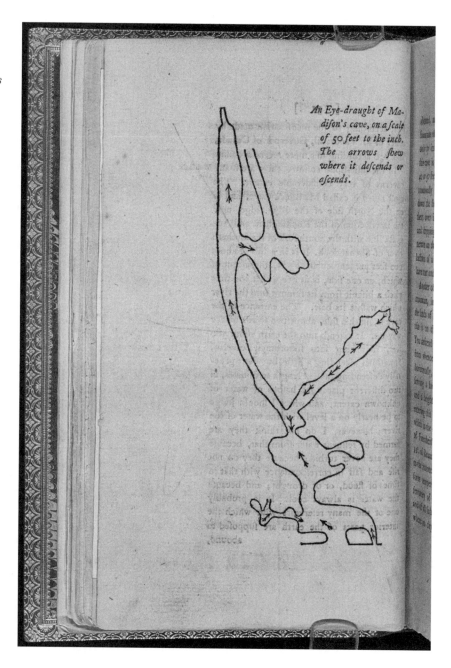

year, and stated those averages in the following table, adding an analytical view of the winds during the same period.[18]

He goes on to discuss other local climatic fluctuations within the commonwealth. He also briefly reviews his observations and opinions on climate change, which were largely based on prevailing and erroneous theories that were soon to be contested by Noah Webster Jr.[19]

Query VIII deals with population, and Jefferson gives tabular data from 1670 to 1782, with numbers indicating settlers imported, census of inhabitants, and census of tithes. He explains how the figures were obtained and discusses some of their limitations. He attempts to extrapolate his findings to policy considerations pertaining to future growth, noting that the "present desire of America is to produce rapid population by as great importations of foreigners as possible. But is this founded in good policy?"[20]

Query XI, entitled "Aborgines," is intended as a "description of the Indians established in that state?" Here he writes, "When the first effectual settlement of our colony was made . . . the country from the sea-coast to the mountains, and from Patowmac to the most southern waters of James river, was occupied by upwards of forty different tribes of Indians." Jefferson describes the various territories of the Powhatans, Mannahoacs, and Monacans. He also provides detailed tabular information outlining the geographical dispersions of the major tribal groups and entertains questions of Native American origins within the more expansive boundaries of North and South America, referencing the already well-known landmark voyages of James Cook:

> Great question has arisen from whence came those aboriginal inhabitants of America? Discoveries, long ago made, were sufficient to shew that a passage from Europe to America was always practicable, even to the imperfect navigation of ancient times. In going from Norway to Iceland, from Iceland to Groenland, from Groenland to Labrador, the first traject is the widest: and this having been practised from the earliest times of which we have any account of that part of the earth, it is not difficult to suppose that the subsequent trajects may have been sometimes passed. Again, the late discoveries of Captain Cook, coasting from Kamschatka to California, have proved that, if the two continents of Asia and America be separated at all, it is only by a narrow streight. So that

from this side also, inhabitants may have passed into America: and the resemblance between the Indians of America and the Eastern inhabitants of Asia, would induce us to conjecture, that the former are the descendants of the latter, or the latter of the former: excepting indeed the Eskimaux, who, from the same circumstance of resemblance, and from identity of language, must be derived from the Groenlanders, and these probably from some of the northern parts of the old continent.[21]

Query XII was intended as a "notice of the counties, cities, townships, and villages?" Jefferson first observes that he has provided a list of counties in Query IX, pertaining to military force. He then expands the discussion of counties, noting that they "are 74 in number, of very unequal size and population. Of these 35 are on the tide waters, or in that parallel; 23 are in the Midlands, between the tide waters and Blue ridge of mountains; 8 between the Blue ridge and Alleghaney; and 8 westward of the Alleghaney."[22]

Query XIII, on the "constitution of the state, and its several charters," begins with a discussion of the travels of Sir Walter Raleigh:

Queen Elizabeth by her letters-patent, bearing date March 25, 1584, licensed Sir Walter Raleigh to search for remote heathen lands, not inhabited by Christian people, and granted to him, in fee simple, all the soil within 200 leagues of the places where his people should, within 6 years, make their dwellings or abidings; reserving only, to herself and her successors, their allegiance and one fifth part of all the gold and silver ore they should obtain. Sir Walter immediately sent out two ships which visited Wococon island in North Carolina, and the next year dispatched seven with 107 men, who settled in Roanoke island, about latitude 35°.50'.[23]

Queries XVII (Religion), XVIII (Manners), XIX (Manufactures), and XX (Subjects of Commerce) all have some geographical component to their discussions.

MR. JEFFERSON'S MAP

Notes on the State of Virginia contains Jefferson's only published printed map (fig. 1)—*A Map of the country between Albemarle Sound, and Lake*

Erie, comprehending the whole of Virginia, Maryland, Delaware and Pennsylvania—which was produced specifically for the treatise. He considered the map essential from both intellectual and commercial perspectives.[24] Before settling on British engraver Samuel Neele to handle the production of the English edition of the book, Jefferson had considered, among others, master engraver and publisher William Faden. Jefferson rejected Faden's bid, thinking it too high, and settled for a less-expensive option. In hindsight, based on the ensuing cost overruns that resulted from the correction of numerous engraving errors attributable to Neele's efforts, Jefferson might well have regretted his choice.[25] Neele's work did need substantial correction: Jefferson noted more than 170 errors with another third of the map yet to proof. The Parisian engraver Guillaume Delahaye corrected the plate for the French translation of *Notes*. John Stockdale, publisher of the English edition, also used the Delahaye plate.[26]

Jefferson's map is considered the best map of Virginia from that time. It was not based on an original survey, but rather was a compilation of existing cartographic data from what Jefferson considered to be the most accurate sources.[27] He used Philadelphia as the location for the prime meridian, a common convention.[28] The map demonstrated Jefferson's ideas about the western boundaries of the state and the relative locations of five new states.

Although Jefferson had no previous experience as a mapmaker, he had drawn land survey plats and architectural plans. Both of those activities required certain skills that would help him prepare the map for his book, principal among these an understanding of the concept of scale. It is tempting to speculate that he had learned specific mapmaking skills from his father, but Thomas was only about eight years old when the Fry-Jefferson map appeared, and it is difficult to assert—and impossible to substantiate—that his father trained him for that specific type of task.

For the Pennsylvania portion of his map, Jefferson relied on the work of William Scull, which was first published in 1770 and subsequently appeared in various forms during the following decade, both in Thomas Jefferys's *The American Atlas: Or, A Geographical Description Of The Whole Continent Of America* and William Faden's *The North American Atlas, selected from the Most Authentic Maps, Charts, Plans &c. hitherto published* (fig. 11).[29]

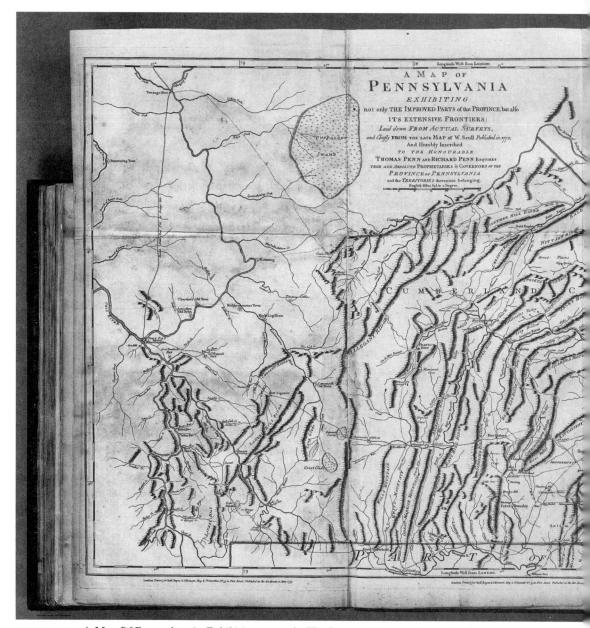

FIGURE 11. *A Map Of Pennsylvania Exhibiting not only The Improved Parts of that Province, but also Its Extensive Frontiers: Laid down From Actual Surveys, and Chiefly From The Late Map of W. Scull Published in 1770,* by William Scull, published by Sayer and Bennett, London, 1776, in Jefferys's *American Atlas.* This particular atlas was a favorite of Jefferson's, and although it cannot be certain which variant of the Scull map he used, this particular issue is a reasonable possibility. (David Rumsey Map Collection)

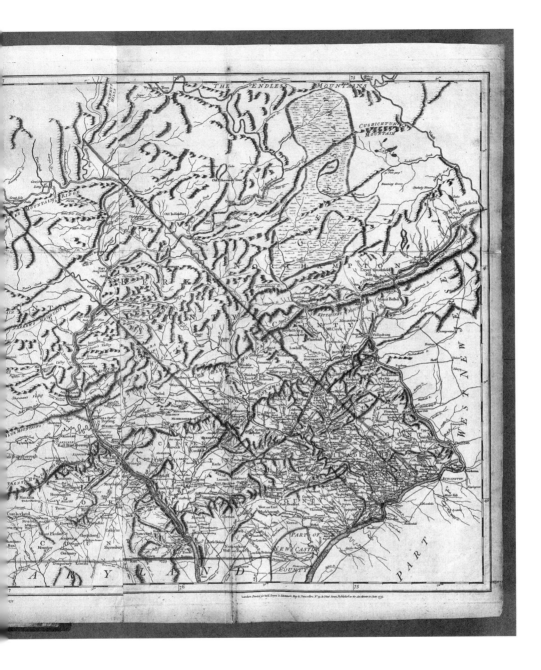

London, Printed for Robt. Sayer & Jn. Bennett, Map & Print sellers, No. 53, in Fleet Street, Published as the Act directs 10 June 1775.

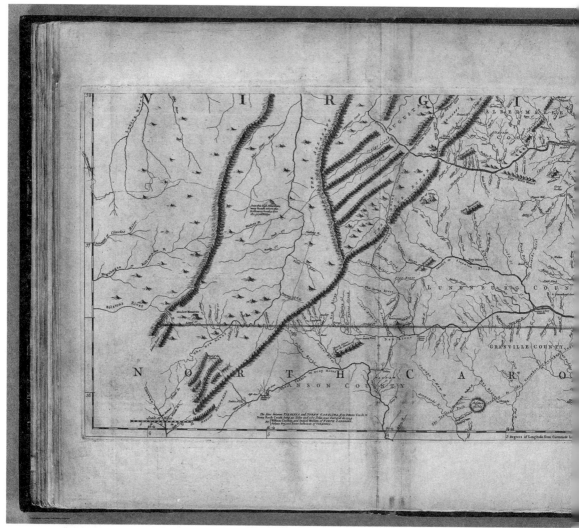

FIGURE 12. *A Map of the most Inhabited part of Virginia containing the whole province of Maryland with Part of Pensilvania, New Jersey and North Carolina. Drawn by Joshua Fry & Peter Jefferson,* by Thomas Jefferys (southern section only), published by Sayer and Bennett, London, 1776, in Jeffery's *American Atlas.* Given Thomas Jefferson's penchant for up-to-date material, it is likely he used this later variant for *Notes on the State of Virginia.* (David Rumsey Map Collection)

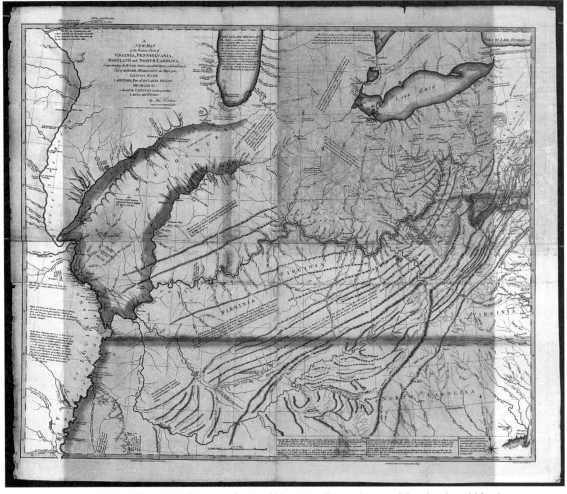

FIGURE 13. *A New Map of the Western Parts of Virginia, Pennsylvania, Maryland and North Carolina; Comprehending the River Ohio, and all the Rivers, which fall into it; Part of the River Mississippi, the Whole of the Illinois River, Lake Erie; Part of the Lakes Huron, Michigan &c. And all the Country bordering on these Lakes and Rivers,* by Thomas Hutchins, 1778. (Albert and Shirley Small Special Collections Library, University of Virginia)

FIGURE 14. *An Accurate Map Of North And South Carolina With Their Indian Frontiers, Shewing in a distinct manner all the Mountains, Rivers, Swamps, Marshes, Bays, Creeks, Harbours, Sandbanks and Soundings on the Coasts; with The Roads and Indian Paths; as well as The Boundary or Provincial Lines, The Several Townships and other divisions of the Land In Both The Provinces; the whole From Actual Surveys By Henry Mouzon And Others,* by Thomas Jefferys (western section only), published by Sayer and Bennett, London, 1776, in Jefferys's *American Atlas.* (Albert and Shirley Small Special Collections Library, University of Virginia)

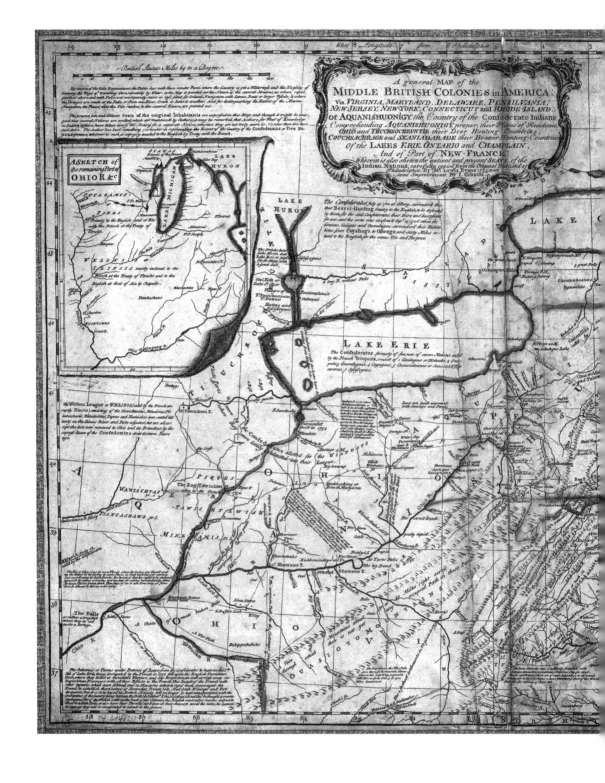

A general MAP of the
MIDDLE BRITISH COLONIES in AMERICA,
Viz. VIRGINIA, MARYLAND, DELAWARE, PENSILVANIA,
NEW JERSEY, NEW YORK, CONNECTICUT and RHODE ISLAND:
Of AQUANISHUONÍGY the Country of the Confederate Indians;
Comprehending AQUANISHUONIGY proper, their Places of Residence,
OHIO and THUCHSOCHRUNTIE their Deer Hunting Countries;
COUCHSACHRAGE and SKANIADARADE their Beaver Hunting Countries;
Of the LAKES ERIE, ONTARIO and CHAMPLAIN,
And of Part of NEW FRANCE;
Wherein is also shewn the antient and present SEATS of the
Indian Nations, carefully copied from the Original Publish'd at
Philadelphia. By Mr. LEWIS EVANS 1755, with
some Improvements by I. GIBSON.

A SKETCH of
the remaining Part of
OHIO R. &c.

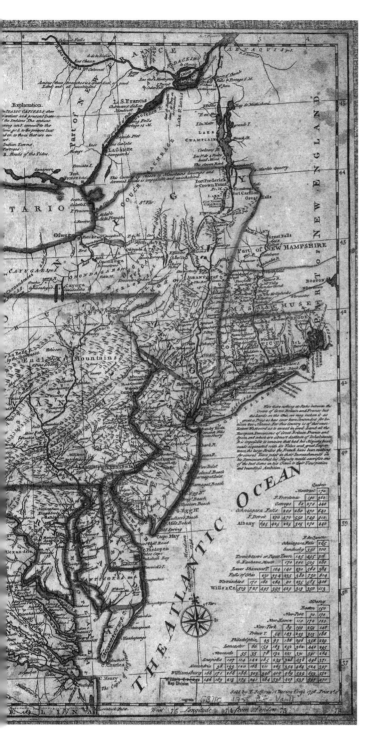

FIGURE 15.

A general map of the middle British colonies in America: Viz. Virginia, Maryland, Delaware, Pensilvania, New-Jersey, New-York, Connecticut and Rhode-Island: Of Aquanishuonigy the country of the confederate Indians comprehending Aquanishuonigy proper, their places of residence, Ohio and Thuchsochruntie their deer hunting countries, Couchsachrage and Skaniadarade their beaver hunting countries, of the Lakes Erie, Ontario and Champlain, and of part of New France: Wherein is also shewn the antient and present seats of the Indian nations; carefully copied from the original published at Philadelphia, by Mr. Lewis Evans 1755, with some improvements by I. Gibson, published by Thomas Jefferys, London, 1758. (American Memory Collection, Library of Congress)

The Virginia section of the map was largely predicated on the Fry-Jefferson *Map of the most Inhabited part of Virginia containing the whole province of Maryland with Part of Pensilvania, New Jersey and North Carolina,* first published circa 1753 by Thomas Jefferys in London (fig. 12).[30] Jefferson felt he needed more recent information for the western part of the state, and turned to Thomas Hutchins's 1778 publication, *A New Map of the Western Parts of Virginia, Pennsylvania, Maryland, and North Carolina* (fig. 13).[31] Additional sources likely used for reference included Henry Mouzon's 1775 imprint, *An Accurate Map Of North And South Carolina With Their Indian Frontiers, Shewing in a distinct manner all the Mountains, Rivers, Swamps, Marshes, Bays, Creeks, Harbours, Sandbanks and Soundings on the Coasts* (fig. 14), and Lewis Evan's seminal 1755 work, *A general Map of the middle British Colonies in America: Viz. Virginia, Maryland, Delaware, Pensilvania, New-Jersey, New-York, Connecticut and Rhode-Island* (fig. 15).[32]

Jefferson kept his own notes on how to begin the drafting process:

1. Lay down Delaware from Newcastle to 40°.15′ from Rittenhouse fixing Philadelphia 39°.56′.29″.4
2. Mason and Dixon's line to Dunkarder
3. St. Clair and McLean: north line which fixes Pittsburgh
4. Ohio to gr. Kanhaway from Hutchins and Hooper
5. The southern boundary from Sharp rock cr by Walker and Smith
6. Fill intermediate spaces from the works of Todd, Evans, etc.
7. The Eastern shore from Churchman's map
8. The country about Hampton and Portsmouth, Andrews.

Lat of Wmsbgh from Mr. Madison
Lat of Monticello my own observations, 38°.8′.17″[33]

Although Jefferson also relied on his own observations, in addition to the cartographic works noted above, this was not sufficient for his purposes. He received relevant geographical information from the likes of John Page (later the thirteenth governor of Virginia), David Rittenhouse (a prominent American astronomer, mathematician, and surveyor), and Francis Hopkinson (a writer and pamphleteer who was a New Jersey delegate to the Continental Congress and an original signer of the Declaration of Independence). Jefferson wrote to Hopkinson from Paris in August of 1786:

I will send, as you propose, copies of my Notes to the Philosophical society, and the City library as soon as I shall have received a map which I have constructed for them, and which is now engraving. This will be a map of the country from Albemarle sound to Lake Erie, as exact as the materials hitherto published would enable me to make it, and brought into a single sheet. I have with great impatience hoped to receive from some of my friends a particular description of the Southern and Western limits of Pennsylvania. Perhaps it might still come in time if you could send it to me in the moment almost of your receiving this. Indeed it would be very desirable if you could only write me an answer to these two queries, viz. How far Westward of F. Pitt does the Western line of Pennsylvania pass? At what point of the river Ohio does 250 that line strike it? Should this arrive even after they shall have begun to strike off the map, I can have the plate altered so as that the latter copies shall give that line right.[34]

Notes on the State of Virginia remains at least as much a landmark geographical treatise as a political work. The accompanying regional map of contemporary Virginia, a historical document in its own right, was a fitting complement to the whole and not just a superfluous illustration. And it was merely one of Jefferson's projects: he worked on the manuscript and map while he was living in Paris as commissioner and minister to France, at the same time he was building his Great Library, which would in time become the foundation of the Library of Congress.

3

LIBRARY OF THE
GEOGRAPHY OF AMERICA

❀ ❀ ❀
❀ ❀
❀

Jefferson's commitment to books, and hence to education and learning, is legendary.[1] His "Great Library," the basis for the reconstitution of the Library of Congress after it had been torched by British troops in 1814, was a product of decades of sustained and painstaking effort. As he recollected in a letter to a contemporary:

> You know my collection, its condition and extent. I have been fifty years making it, and have spared no pains, opportunity or expense, to make it what it is. While residing in Paris [as minister to France], I devoted every afternoon I was disengaged, for a summer or two, in examining all the principal bookstores, turning over every book with my own hand, and putting by everything which related to America, and indeed whatever was rare and valuable in every science. Besides this, I had standing orders during the whole time I was in Europe, on its principal book-marts, particularly Amsterdam, Frankfort, Madrid and London, for such works relating to America as could not be found in Paris. So that in that department particularly, such a collection was made as probably can never again be effected, because it is hardly probable that the same opportunities, the same time, industry, perseverance and expense, with some knowledge of the bibliography of the subject, would again happen to be in concurrence. During the same period, and after my return to America, I was led to procure, also, whatever related to the duties of those in the high concerns of the nation. So that the collection, which I suppose is of between nine and ten thousand volumes, while it includes what is chiefly valuable in science and literature generally, extends more particularly to whatever belongs to the American statesman. . . . It is long since

I have been sensible it ought not to continue private property . . .
Congress should have the refusal of it at their own price. . . . I ask
of your friendship, therefore, to make for me the tender of it to the
library committee of Congress. . . . I enclose you the catalogue,
which will enable them to judge of its contents. . . . I do not know
that it contains any branch of science which Congress would wish
to exclude from their collection; there is, in fact, no subject to
which a member of Congress may not have occasion to refer. . . .
My desire is either to place it in their hands entire, or to preserve
it so here. I am engaged in making an alphabetical index of the
author's names, to be annexed to the catalogue, which I will
forward to you as soon as completed.[2]

Even before he offered to sell his expansive library to Congress, Jefferson's commitment to the early development of the Library of Congress is clearly evident:

I have prepared a catalogue for the Library of Congress in
conformity with your ideas that books of entertainment are not
within the scope of it, and that books in other languages, where
there are not translations of them, are not to be admitted freely.
I have confined the catalogue to those branches of science which
belong to the deliberations of the members as statesmen.[3]

That 1802 list specified books to be purchased in both London and
Paris, and included a geography subheading that comprised not only
dictionaries and atlases, but also numerous history texts related to the
subject.

Libraries in colonial America were not large by modern standards.
A collection of two hundred volumes was considered substantial. One
of the largest seventeenth-century private libraries, owned by the Reverend Cotton Mather, was estimated by his son to have included seven
to eight thousand volumes.[4] Jefferson's collection, which he amassed
during the latter half of the eighteenth century and sold to Congress in
1814 for $23,950, numbered roughly 6,700 volumes.[5] By contrast, John
Adams owned slightly more than 2,700 volumes.[6]

In the fastidious collection and organization of his Great Library,
Jefferson shines as a collector, curator, and cataloger. As a collector, his
interests were not specifically antiquarian, and his goal was frequently

to obtain the most up-to-date information possible on a given subject; that necessarily included but was not confined to early works. Contrary to most libraries in colonial Virginia,[7] Jefferson's included substantial holdings in history and travel accounts. He also had extensive—and at times related—volumes pertaining to geography, with some clear and detailed focus on the exploration of the Americas. The library he sold to Congress in 1814 had roughly three hundred items classified under "geography," dwarfing the forty-three listed under architecture.[8]

The small library he inherited from his father contained but a few titles related to geography, together with several maps.[9] Jefferson's organizational strategy and intellectual emphasis developed over a period of decades, and appears to have substantially coalesced by the time of his 1783 catalog, where geography is classified under philosophy, and more specifically under the physico-mathematical subsection.[10] Not all of his holdings pertaining to geographical considerations were confined to the specific subheading, and various titles focused on such subjects as astronomy, surveying, and history also contain relevant content.[11] Jefferson's specific reasons for ordering his geographical entries may never be entirely clear, although there is distinct evidence of a personal organizational style that was not simply alphabetical or chronological, but also considered geographical and subject associations.[12]

Jefferson's library was not confined to books, and included many maps not readily apparent in published lists of his holdings.[13] When he purchased maps during his years in Paris, he often did not list them by specific titles, nor did he consistently note the geographic region displayed.[14]

In terms of specific titles (which would prove too lengthy to list here), the first ten items Jefferson notes in his own classification of general geography are as follows:

1. Dionysii orbis Descriptio
2. Dionysii Geographia
3. Strabo, Gr. Lat. Casauboni
4. Pomponius Mela de Situ Orbis.
5. Solinus Polyhistor, 12° Lipsiae
6. Cluverii Geographia
7. Veteris orbis Tabula Geographicae, Amstelodami, Covens et Mortier

9. Atlas portatif de Grenet et Bonne
10. Atlas by Arrowsmith and Lewis

With respect to Jefferson's section on American geography, the initial ten listings are:

1. Ortelii Theatrum Orbis
2. Jeffery's American Atlas
3. Atlas Americain de Rouge
4. Morse's American Geography
5. Morse's American Gazetteer
6. Tableau des Etats Unis par Pictet.
7. Birch's views of Philadelphia
8. The English Pilot, fourth book
9. Description des Cotes de l'Amerique, par Dassie
10. Recherches sur les Americains, par Paw[15]

It is difficult to determine which titles Jefferson most often used or considered important, and they likely varied over the decades. Other significant geographic works he owned and consulted include the following:

- Stith's *The History of the First Discovery and Settlement of Virginia: Being an Essay towards a General History of this Colony;*
- Three of Hennepin's works including *Description de la Louisiane, nouvellement decouverte au sud oüest de la Nouvelle France, Nouvelle Decouverte d' un tres Grand Pays situé dans l'Amerique,* and *Nouvelle Voyage d'un Pais plus grande que L'Europe;*
- Charlevoix's *Histoire et description générale de la Nouvelle France, avec le journal historique d'un voyage fait par ordre du roi dans l'Amerique Septentrionnale;*
- Page du Pratz's *History of Louisisana Or Of The Western Parts Of Virginia And Carolina: Containing A Description Of The Countries That Lie On Both Sides Of The River Missisippi;*
- Catesby's *Natural History of Carolina, Florida and the Bahama Islands;*
- Hutchins's *A Topographical Description of Virginia, Pennsylvania, Maryland, and North Carolina;*

- Carver's *Three Years Travels Throughout The Interior Parts Of North-America, For More Than Five Thousand Miles;*
- Jefferys's *The Natural and Civil History of the French Dominions in North and South America;*
- Cook's *Voyage to the Pacific Ocean, undertaken by the Command of His Majesty, for making discoveries in the Northern Hemisphere;*
- Purchas's *Purchas his pilgrimage, or Relations of the World and the Religions observed in all ages and places discovered, from the Creation unto this Present;*
- Mackenzie's *Voyages from Montreal on the River St. Laurence Through the Continent of North America to the Frozen and Pacific Oceans in the Years 1789 and 1793, with a Preliminary Account of the Rise, Progress, and Present State of the Fur Trade of That Country;*
- Several volumes of the de Bry voyages, and numerous others.[16]

Many of these titles—preeminently focused on the expanding geographical knowledge of America—were crucial to his personal education and his presidential role as one of the great expedition planners of his era.

4

JEFFERSON AS EXPEDITION PLANNER

❊ ❊ ❊
❊ ❊
❊

Thomas Jefferson's Grand Tour of Europe was not mirrored by personal travels to the western reaches of the North American continent. There is little indication he was motivated to journey to those as yet poorly explored landscapes. Yet despite the fact that he never ventured west of the town of Staunton, Virginia—nestled on the western edge of the Shenandoah Valley—he is still considered one of the great expedition planners of his day. This short list also includes England's great naturalist, Sir Joseph Banks, who traveled with Captain James Cook on his first voyage, and Sir Alexander Mackenzie, the Scottish-born Canadian fur trader and explorer.[1] Jefferson's own continental vision looked over and far beyond those Virginia ridges.

Jefferson never met Banks or Mackenzie, but the latter's *Voyages from Montreal,* first published in 1801, was a driving force in his final push to have the Pacific Northwest explored during his presidency, which led to the landmark expedition of Meriwether Lewis and William Clark.[2] Fear that the British would follow Mackenzie's advice and expand more forcefully into those regions was a major part of Jefferson's motivation. Yet the reasons for national sponsorship of eighteenth-century geographic exploration went beyond conquest and imperial expansion, and involved additional and complex interplays of commercial, scientific, and political goals.[3]

This chapter considers Jefferson's role as expedition planner, with particular attention to his involvement in setting frameworks for exploration of the Pacific Northwest and other parts of the Louisiana Purchase.

It is difficult to pinpoint the precise moment when exploration of this region became a major concern for Jefferson. Like so many others, he was focused on finding the fabled Northwest Passage.[4] In an oft-quoted letter to George Rogers Clark on 4 December 1783, he writes:

> I find they have subscribed a very large sum of money in England for exploring the country from the Missisipi to California. They pretend it is only to promote knolege. I am afraid they have thoughts of colonising into that quarter. Some of us have been talking here in a feeble way of making the attempt to search that country. But I doubt whether we have enough of that kind of spirit to raise the money.[5]

Clark agreed with the need for the mission but declined to lead it, although he offered to provide what aid he could should a future exploration be possible. He also offered some advice to Jefferson:

> Should Congress resolve to have the western Country Explored I should take pleasure in lending all the aid in my power as an Individual it is what I think we ought to do. But pardon me when I inform you that I think our Ideas of this Business is generally wrong. Large parties will never answer the purpose. They will allarm the Indian Nations they pass through. Three or four young Men well qualified for the Task might perhaps compleat your wishes at a very Trifling Expence a tolerable subsistance on their return might procure them. They must learn the Language of the distant Nations they pass through, the Geography of their Country, antient Speech or Tradition, passing as men tracing the steps of our four Fathers wishing to know from whence we came. This would require four or five years, an Expence worthey the attention of Congress, from the Nature of things I should suppose that you would require a general superintendant of Indian affairs to the westward as the greatest body of those people live in that quarter.[6]

Hard on the heels of these communications, and shortly after his move to France as a commissioner to help negotiate commercial treaties—and eventually as minister to that nation—Jefferson met John

Ledyard, an American who had been a member of the crew on Captain James Cook's third voyage, which secretly searched for the fabled Northwest Passage. Ledyard was the first U.S. citizen to land in the Pacific Northwest and write about it.[7] Jefferson had hoped the explorer would lead an expedition into the northwestern parts of North America, but Ledyard died before anything could be organized:

> A country man of ours, a Mr. Lediard of Connecticut set out
> from hence some time ago for St. Petersburgh, to go thence to
> Kamschatka, thence to cross over to the Western coast of America,
> and penetrate through the continent to our side of it. He had got
> within a few days journey of Kamschatka, when he was arrested
> by order of the empress of Russia, sent back and turned adrift
> in Poland. He went to London, engaged under the auspices of a
> private society formed there for pushing discoveries into Africa,
> passed by this place, which he left a few days ago for Marseilles,
> where he will embark for Alexandria and Grand Cairo, thence
> explore the Nile to it's source, cross to the head of the Niger, and
> descend that to it's mouth. He promises me, if he escapes through
> this journey, he will go to Kentuckey and endeavour to penetrate
> Westwardly from thence to the South sea.[8]

Jefferson was also familiar with Jean-François de Galaup, Comte de Lapérouse, another crew member on Cook's third voyage. Lapérouse had been charged by Louis XVI to continue the search for the ever-elusive Northwest Passage, and in language resembling the concerns he had expressed to George Rogers Clark in 1783, Jefferson wrote to John Jay on 14 August 1785:

> You have doubtless seen in the papers that this court was
> sending two vessels into the South sea, under the conduct of a
> Capt. Peyrouse. They give out that the object is merely for the
> improvement of our knowlege of the geography of that part of
> the globe. And certain it is that they carry men of eminence in
> different branches of science. Their loading however as detailed
> in conversations and some other circumstances appeared to me
> to indicate some other design: perhaps that of colonising on the
> Western coast of America, or perhaps only to establish one or

more factories there for the fur trade. We may be little interested in either of these objects. But we are interested in another, that is, to know whether they are perfectly weaned from the desire of possessing continental colonies in America.[9]

The next "training leg" for Jefferson's interests in the exploration of the Pacific Northwest involved the never-realized attempt of French diplomat and botanist André Michaux to head the mission. He had been sent to the United States in 1785 by Louis XVI, initially to find botanical species that would be of use to France. In 1791 he proposed a plan for westward expansion to the American Philosophical Society. By early 1793, Jefferson, as secretary of state under George Washington, was attempting to raise funds to finance that hoped-for expedition, culminating in the mission instructions issued by the Society, which he had written:

> Sundry persons having subscribed certain sums of money for your encouragement to explore the country along the Missouri, and thence Westwardly to the Pacific ocean, having submitted the plan of the enterprize to the direction of the American Philosophical society, and the Society having accepted of the trust, they proceed to give you the following instructions.
>
> They observe to you that the chief objects of your journey are to find the shortest and most convenient route of communication between the US. and the Pacific ocean, within the temperate latitudes, and to learn such particulars as can be obtained of the country through which it passes, it's productions, inhabitants and other interesting circumstances.
>
> As a channel of communication between these states and the Pacific ocean, the Missouri, so far as it extends, presents itself under circumstances of unquestioned preference. It has therefore been declared as a fundamental object of the subscription, (not to be dispensed with) that this river shall be considered and explored as a part of the communication sought for . . .
>
> You will, in the course of your journey, take notice of the country you pass through, it's general face, soil, rivers, mountains, it's productions animal, vegetable, and mineral so far as they may be new to us and may also be useful or very curious; the latitude of

places or materials for calculating it by such simple methods as your situation may admit you to practice, the names, numbers, and dwellings of the inhabitants, and such particularities as you can learn of their history, connection with each other, languages, manners, state of society and of the arts and commerce among them.[10]

Michaux never pursued the mission, as his plans apparently changed suddenly under the influence of Edmond-Charles Genêt ("Citizen Genêt"), French ambassador to the United States during the French Revolution. Some have even accused Michaux of spying on the United States for Genêt, but that has never been proven. Jefferson was aware of at least some of Michaux's dealings with the French ambassador.[11]

By this time Jefferson was almost certainly the most well-read American with respect to available, published information concerning the geography and general lore of Pacific Northwest. His Great Library, as noted in the preceding chapter, was a testament to his efforts to gather as much "useful knowledge" as possible. No other American had a finer collection of relevant literature.[12]

Shortly before President Jefferson's Northwest expeditionary proposal was approved by Congress in February 1803, he was involved with the inception of another crucial institution that would profoundly influence the future geographic and cartographic activities of the expanding republic: the 1802 founding of the United States Military Academy at West Point. The initial step in the founding of the academy had been the 1794 act of Congress establishing the "Corps of Artillerists and Engineers" with the army.[13] This eventually led to establishment of the Corps of Engineers in 1802, creating the first engineering school in the United States at West Point.

In a secret message to Congress on 18 January 1803, in which Jefferson requested $2,500 for the expedition, he observed:

The river Missouri, and the Indians inhabiting it, are not as well known as is rendered desirable by their connexion with the Mississippi, and consequently with us. It is, however, understood, that the country on that river is inhabited by numerous tribes, who furnish great supplies of furs and peltry to the trade of another nation, carried on in a high latitude, through an infinite number of portages and lakes, shut up by ice through a long season. The commerce on that line could bear no competition with that of the Missouri, traversing a moderate climate, offering according to the best accounts, a continued navigation from its source, and possibly with a single portage, from the Western Ocean, and finding to the Atlantic a choice of channels through the Illinois or Wabash, the lakes and Hudson, through the Ohio and Susquehanna, or Potomac or James rivers, and through the Tennessee and Savannah, rivers. An intelligent officer, with ten or twelve chosen men . . . might explore the whole line, even to the Western Ocean, have conferences with the natives on the subject of commercial intercourse . . . and return with the information acquired, in the course of two summers . . . While other civilized nations have encountered great expense to enlarge the boundaries of knowledge by undertaking voyages of discovery, and for other literary purposes, in various parts and directions, our nation seems to owe to the same object, as well as to its own interests, to explore this, the only line of easy communication across the continent, and so directly traversing our own part of it.[14]

Jefferson clearly understood the importance of river navigation and charting both for future exploration and commerce.

During the intense planning of the Lewis and Clark expedition, one of the most important elements was the amassing and assessment of the most up-to-date maps available of the Pacific Northwest.[15] On 14 March 1803, Albert Gallatin, secretary of the treasury and a man also well versed in the importance of geography and cartography, wrote to Jefferson:

Capn. Lewis leaves this place to morrow morning. I have requested Mr. King to project a blank map to extend from 88 to 126° West longitude from Greenwich & from 30° to 55° north latitude; which will give us the whole course of the Mississipi Maps and the whole coast of the Pacific ocean within the same latitudes together with a sufficient space to the North to include all the head waters of the Port Nelson River. In this I intend to insert the course of the Mississipi Maps as high up as the Ohio Maps from Ellicot's, the coast of the Pacific from Cook & Vancouver, the north bend of the Missouri Maps & such other of its waters as are there delineated from the three maps of Arrowsmith & from that of Mackenzie, and the Rio Norte and other parts of the Missoury from Danville & Delisle. The most difficult point to ascertain is the latitude of the sources of the Rio Norte: and it is important, in order to know whether there would be any danger in following a more southerly branch of the Missouri Maps than that delineated in Mackenzie's & in the manuscript transcribed from Mr. Thornton's map by Cap. Lewis. I mention this because you may perhaps have some book at Monticello, which might throw some light on that subject or at least on the latitude & longitude of Santa Fe Maps.[16]

Jefferson replied on 20 March 1803:

I do not find in my library any thing which can throw light on the geography of the Rio Norte. I do not believe that in modern times any thing has been added to the information as to that river in early times. of this information Mitchell had the benefit. his map was made under public patronage & with all the information that could procure him. that it was made with great care we know from what is laid down in those Western parts with which we have lately become accustomed. Certainly his map we find much nearer the truth than could have been expected considering when it was made. Hence I conclude that his delineation of the Rio Norte is more to be credited than any other, not excepting Danville & Delisle.[17]

On 13 April 1803, Gallatin wrote to Jefferson about his proposed instructions for the Lewis and Clark expedition:

But whatever may be the issue of the present difficulties, the future destinies of the Missouri country are of vast importance to the United States, it being perhaps the only large tract of country, and certainly the first which lying out of the boundaries of the Union will be settled by the people of the U. States. The precise extent, therefore, of the country drained by all the waters emptying into that river, and consequently the length & directions of all the principal branches ought to be, as far as practicable, ascertained as well as that particular branch which may be followed for the purpose of examining the communications with the Pacific Ocean. That tract of country is bounded on the north by the Waters of Hudson's bay, the extent of which southwardly is tolerably ascertained by Mackenzie & others; Westwardly by the Waters of the Columbia & other rivers emptying into the Pacific, which it is the principal object of this voyage to explore; and Southwardly, it is presumed, by the waters of Rio Norte. How far these extend Northwardly & confine the waters of the Missouri it is important to know, as their position would generally determine the extent of territory watered by the Missouri Maps. It is presumable, from analogy that the Waters of Hudson's bay which interlock with the many northerly streams of the Missouri are divided from them by elevated lands interspersed with lakes, but not by any regular chain of mountains. By the same analogy, (for within the United States & known parts of North America the spring of every river north of 42° latitude issues from a lake, and south of 41° from a mountain,) it is probable that the northern branches of the Rio Norte are separated from the southern streams of the Kanses & Missouri rivers by a chain of mountains running westwardly till it unites with the chain which divides the waters of Missouri & other rivers from those emptying into the Pacific. Hence it is presumable that the distance of that east & west chain from the Missouri will generally show the extent of country watered by this river. And although Cn L. [Captain Lewis] going westwardly toward his main object may not personally become acquainted with the country lying south of his track, yet so far as he may collect information on that subject & also on the communications with the Rio Norte or other southern rivers if any others, which is not probable, interlocks with the Missouri, it would be a desirable object. The great object to ascertain is whether from its extent & fertility that country is susceptible of a large population, in the same manner as the corresponding tract on the Ohio. Besides the general opinion which may be formed of its fertility, some more specific instructions on the signs of the soil might be given—the two principal of which are the prevailing species of timber whether oak-beech-pine-or barren, and the evenness or mountainous & rocky situation of the land. Those two circumstances do generally determine in America the quantity of soil fit for cultivation in any one large tract of country: for I presume there are no swamps in that part of the world.[18]

Shortly thereafter, on 20 June 1803, Jefferson issued his well-known, lengthy, detailed, and oft-quoted instructions to Meriwether Lewis:

Instruments for ascertaining, by celestial observations, the geography of the country through which you will pass, have been already provided. Light articles for barter and presents among the Indians, arms for your attendants, say for from 10. to 12. men, boats, tents, & other travelling apparatus, with ammunition, medecine, surgical instruments and provisions you will have prepared with such aids as the Secretary at War can yield in his department; & from him also you will recieve authority to engage among our troops, by voluntary agreement, the number of attendants above mentioned, over whom you, as their commanding officer, are invested with all the powers the laws give in such a case . . .

The object of your mission is to explore the Missouri river, & such principal stream of it, as, by it's course & communication with the waters of the Pacific Ocean, whether the Columbia, Oregan, Colorado or and other river may offer the most direct & practicable water communication across this continent, for the purposes of commerce.

Beginning at the mouth of the Missouri, you will take careful observations of latitude & longitude, at all remarkeable points on the river, & especially at the mouths of rivers, at rapids, at islands, & other places & objects distinguished by such natural marks & characters of a durable kind, as that they may with certainty be recognised hereafter. The courses of the river between these points of observation may be supplied by the compass the log-line & by time, corrected by the observations themselves. The variations of the compass too, in different places, should be noticed . . .

Altho' your route will be along the channel of the Missouri, yet you will endeavor to inform yourself, by enquiry, of the character & extent of the country watered by it's branches, & especially on it's Southern side. The North river or Rio Bravo which runs into the gulph of Mexico, and the North river, or Rio colorado which runs into the gulph of California, are understood to be the principal streams heading opposite to the waters of the Missouri, and running Southwardly. Whether the dividing grounds between the Missouri & them are mountains or flatlands, what are their distance from the Missouri, the character of the intermediate country, & the people inhabiting it, are worthy of particular enquiry. The Northern waters of the Missouri are less to be enquired after, becaue they have been ascertained to a considerable degree, & are still in a course of ascertainment by English traders, and travellers. But if you can learn any thing certain of the most Northern source of the Missisipi, & of its position relatively to the lake of the woods, it will be interesting to us.[19]

The letters between Gallatin and Jefferson give us a glimpse of the maps used for planning the expedition, and for preparing Nicholas King's 1803 base map (fig. 16).[20] Among the most important of the referenced maps are two early variants—most likely those published in 1795 and 1802—of Aaron Arrowsmith's *A Map Exhibiting all the New Discoveries in the Interior Parts of North America* (fig. 17). The third of the Arrowsmith maps discussed was probably the 1802 version of *A Map of the United States of North America* (fig. 18).[21]

Additional maps referenced in planning the expedition included Alexander Mackenzie's 1801 *A Map of America between Latitudes 40 and 70 North, and Longitudes 45 and 180 West, Exhibiting Mackenzie's Track* (fig. 19). There is mention of several maps by the prominent French mapmakers Jean Baptiste Bourguignon d'Anville and Guillaume Delisle, whose 1718 *Carte de la Louisiane et du Cours du Mississipi* (fig. 20) was one of the preeminent and enduring images of the eighteenth century.[22]

Another map that Jefferson mentioned specifically in his response to Gallatin's early March 1803 letter was John Mitchell's *A Map of the British and French Dominions in North America* (fig. 21). Mitchell was a botanist and physician, and his reputation as a cartographer derives from this, the only map he ever published, which is considered a landmark in the early history of British North America and the United States.[23]

The voluminous correspondence to and from Jefferson concerning geographic and cartographic issues pertaining to the ongoing expedition, which is beyond the scope of this discussion, is reproduced and discussed in a range of published sources.[24]

By the time Jefferson signed the Purchase agreement with the French on 30 April 1803, he was well aware of the importance of the Louisiana Territory, and in particular the implications of exerting control over the entire Mississippi River watershed. Although the price of fifteen million dollars is frequently reckoned a bargain (and it was), the cost is deceptive, because what the United States purchased were the Discovery Rights to an area of land whose borders and interiors were not well known. This was not a fee-simple purchase of an accurately surveyed expanse of territory, and the cost ran many times higher after additional agreements were negotiated with the Native Americans who lived on many of those lands (see chapter 6). Even as Jefferson was planning the Lewis and Clark expedition, he was simultaneously considering the need for skilled and rapid exploration of other parts of the newly acquired Louisiana Territory.[25]

While he was president of the United States, Jefferson wrote his own comprehensive analysis of "The Limits and Bounds of Louisiana." He divided his discussion into several sections: a chronological series of facts relative to Louisiana, limits, and an examination into the boundaries of Louisiana. The latter section is followed by a postscript concerning "The Northern Boundary of Louisiana, Coterminous with the possessions of England."[26]

Jefferson's chronology begins with a 1673 entry referencing the travels of Louis Joliet and Jesuit missionary, Father Jacques Marquette, down the Mississippi River, and ends with a 1783 entry noting Great Britain's cession of "the two Floridas" (Spanish Florida and that portion along the Gulf Coast originally held by France as part of Louisiana) to Spain. Jefferson includes more than thirty-five dated entries, usually with applicable references.[27] His discussion of Louisiana's limits begins with mention of Spanish settlements in 1680 and ends with the French cession of 30 April 1803.[28]

His review of the Louisiana boundaries, the final and lengthiest section, textually expands the outlines of the initial two segments. As he notes at the start:

> THE French having for a century and a half been in possession
> of Canada, and it's inhabitants penetrating to the remote waters

FIGURE 16.
Lewis and Clark base map, with annotations in brown ink by Meriwether Lewis, tracing showing the Mississippi, the Missouri for a short distance above Kansas, Lakes Michigan, Superior, and Winnipeg, and the country onwards to the Pacific, by Nicholas King, manuscript, 1803. (American Memory Collection, Library of Congress)

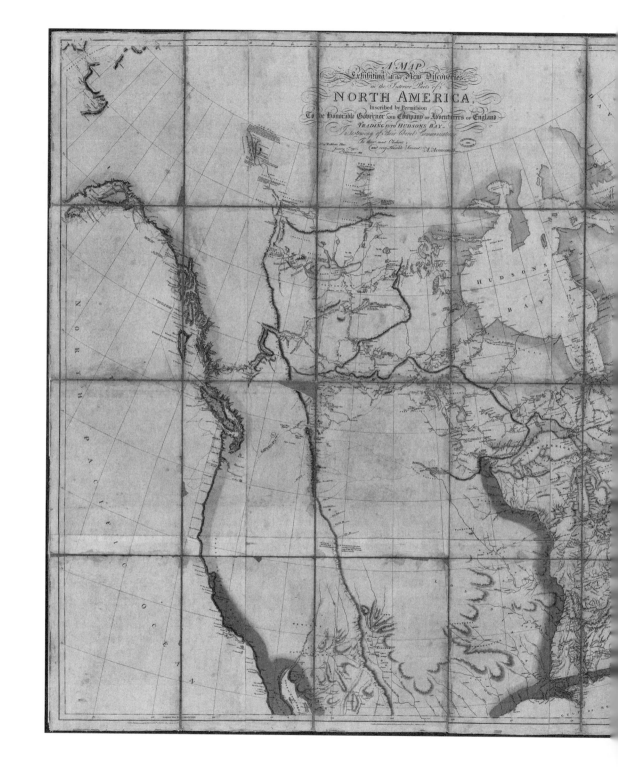

A MAP
Exhibiting all the New Discoveries
in the Interior Parts of
NORTH AMERICA,
Inscribed by Permission
To the Honorable Governor and Company of Adventurers of England
TRADING into HUDSONS BAY.
In testimony of their Liberal Communications

NORTH PACIFIC OCEAN

HUDSON'S BAY

FIGURE 17.

A Map Exhibiting all the new Discoveries in the Interior Parts of North America inscribed by permission to the Honorable Governor and Company of Adventurers of England trading into Hudsons Bay In testimony of their liberal Communications to their most Obedient and very Humble Servant A. Arrowsmith, January 1st 1795, 1802 additions, published by Aaron Arrowsmith, London. (American Memory Collection, Library of Congress)

VIRGINIA

NORTH CAROLINA

CAROLINA

PAMLICO SOUND

ATLANTIC

A MAP OF THE
UNITED STATES
of
NORTH AMERICA
Drawn from a number of Critical Researches
By A. ARROWSMITH,
Hydrographer to H.R.H. the Prince of Wales.
No. 10 SOHO SQUARE

London Published as the Act directs by A. Arrowsmith No. 10 Soho Square. Jan. 1st 1796. Additions 1802.

FIGURE 18.

A Map of the United States of North America. Drawn from a number of critical researches by A. Arrowsmith, Hydrographer to H.R.H. the Prince of Wales (sheet one of four), published by Aaron Arrowsmith, London, 1802. (David Rumsey Map Collection)

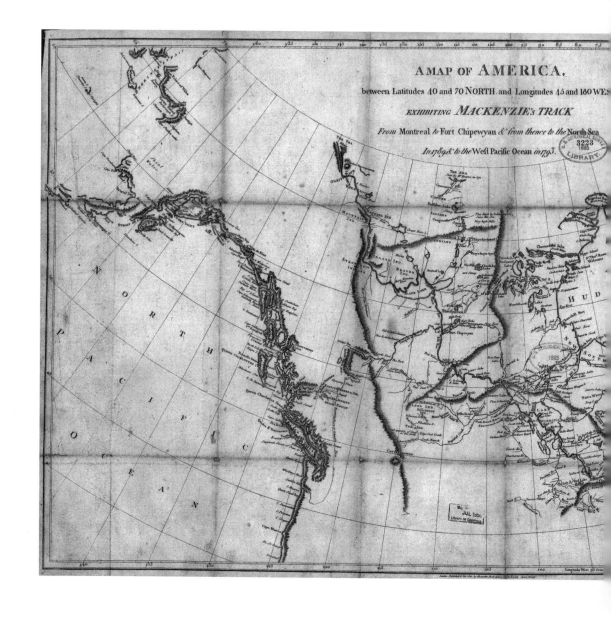

A MAP OF AMERICA,

between Latitudes 40 and 70 NORTH. and Longitudes 45 and 180 WES

EXHIBITING **MACKENZIE's TRACK**

From Montreal *to* Fort Chipewyan & *from thence to the* North Sea

In 1789 & *to the* West Pacific Ocean *in* 1793.

NORTH PACIFIC OCEAN

HUD

London Published at the Act by Alexander Dook &c &c. by Payfield Street Strand

FIGURE 19.

A Map of America between Latitudes 40 and 70 North, and Longitudes 45 and 180 West, Exhibiting Mackenzie's track from Montreal to Fort Chipewyan & from thence to the north sea in 1789 & to the west Pacific Ocean in 1793, by Alexander Mackenzie, published in Mackenzie's *Voyages from Montreal, on the River St. Laurence, through the Continent of North America to the Frozen and Pacific Oceans; In the Years 1789 and 1793,* London, 1801. (American Memory Collection, Library of Congress)

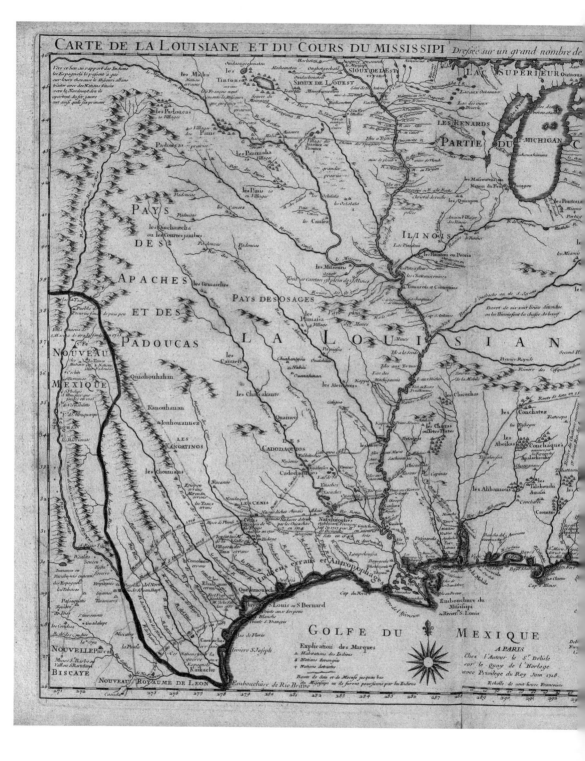

CARTE DE LA LOUISIANE ET DU COURS DU MISSISSIPI *Dressée sur un grand nombre de*

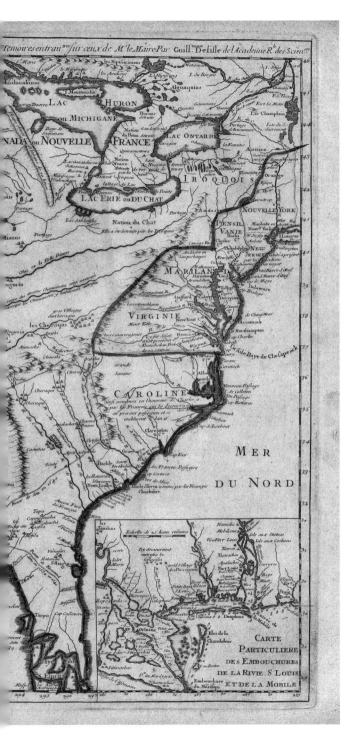

FIGURE 20.

Carte de la Louisiane et du Cours du Mississipi, by Guillaume Delisle. Originally published in Paris in 1718, this variant appeared in 1731. This map, the preeminent view for more than fifty years, was one of the most historically important for the Mississippi Valley. (David Rumsey Map Collection)

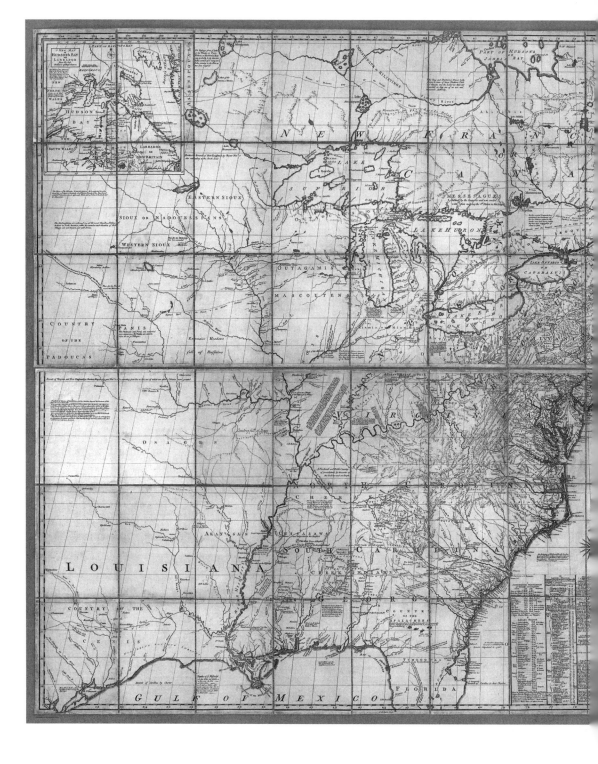

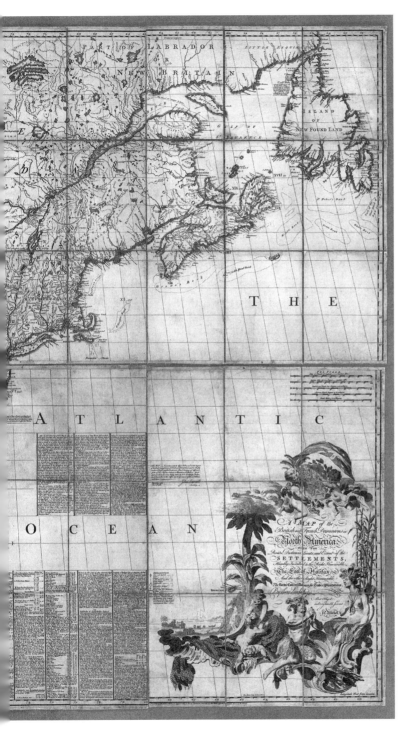

FIGURE 21.

A Map of the British and French Dominions in North America with the Roads, Distances, Limits and Extent of the Settlements, by John Mitchell. Originally published in London in 1755, this variant (2nd edition) was published in 1757. This, Mitchell's only map, with a complex publishing history, is considered one of the most important maps in the history of North America. (David Rumsey Map Collection)

communicating with the S! Laurence, they learned of the Indians that, in the neighborhood of those waters, arose a great river, called the Missisipi, running due South to the sea, and through a fine country unpossessed by any white nation. In 1673. the Sieurs Joliet and Marquette, two Canadians, undertook to explore it, descended the Missisipi as far as the river Arkansa, in 33° & returned to Canada. Their account of it inflamed the enterprize of M. de la Salle, who in 1675, went to France to sollicit authority to explore the MiSsipi. He obtained it, returned to Canada, and in 1680. went as far as the river Illinois, on the lower part of which he built & garrisoned a fort called Crevecoeur, and sent the father Hennepin with 2. men to push his discoveries down the Misipi as far as he could; &, as preparatory to a more formal essay, going himself Northwardly. Hennepin descended the Misipi to the ocean, & returned with the information collected, to the Illinois. In 1682. La Sale & Tonti undertook their expedition; went down the river with 60. men, named the country Louisiana, built a fort in the Chickasaw country, 60 leagues below the Ohio, which they called Prudhomme, reached the ocean, and returned to Canada the ensuing year 1683.[29]

Jefferson goes on to discuss some important details pertaining to the "Rio Norte" (Rio Grande):

Besides being midway between the actual possessions of the two nations, that river formed a natural and well marked boundary, extending very far into the country Northwardly. And accordingly we find by several * maps, some of them published by authority of the French government, and some Spanish maps, that France claimed to that river. This claim has not been abridged, as far as is known, by any public treaty; and those which are secret, if any such have taken place, cannot bind nations having no notice of them, & succeeding fairly to the rights of France, as publicly avowed & believed to exist.[30]

The asterisk in the preceding text refers to a footnote which lists the maps he used in developing his opinions:

I possess three antient maps which mark the Rio bravo & it's Eastern branch as the dividing boundary between Louisiana &

Mexico. 1. Moll's map of the West Indies & adjacent countries. 2. Moll's map of Louisiana etc. published in 1720. in which the Southwestern parts of Louisiana are said to be copied from a French map published in Paris in 1718. and 3. Homann's Spanish map of Louisiana of about the same date.[31]

As noted above, Jefferson included a postscript pertaining to the northern boundary of the territory, which begins as follows:

> THE limits of Louisiana have been spoken of in the preceding statement, as if those established to the West & North, by the charter of Louis XIV. remained still unaltered. In the West they are so, as already explained. But, in the North, a material change has taken place. With this however it was unnecessary to complicate our subject, while considering the interests of Spain alone: because the possessions of Great Britain, & not of Spain, are coterminous with Louisiana on it's Northern boundary. We will now therefore proceed to examine the state of that boundary, as between Gr. Britain & the US.[32]

In addition to the Lewis and Clark expedition, Jefferson played an integral role in the planning of two lesser-known forays into the southeastern regions of the Louisiana Purchase: the Dunbar-Hunter and the Freeman-Custis expeditions. Although Jefferson was aware of Zebulon Pike's journeys into the southwestern reaches of the Purchase, he was not directly involved in planning that mission, which was under the command of General James Wilkinson.[33]

Though the Dunbar-Hunter expedition of the Ouachita River from October 1804 to January 1805 was not as extensive in preparation or scope as Lewis and Clark's mission to the Northwest, Jefferson nonetheless actively participated in its planning.[34] On 13 March 1804, he wrote to Dunbar, a respected natural scientist and merchant living along the Mississippi River near Natchez, Mississippi:

> We were much indebted for your communications on the subject of Louisiana. The substance of what was recieved from you as well as other particulars came, as some were of a nature to excite ill will. Of these publications I sent you a copy. On the subject of the limits of Lousiana nothing was said therein, because we thought it best first to have explanations with Spain. . . . While I was in

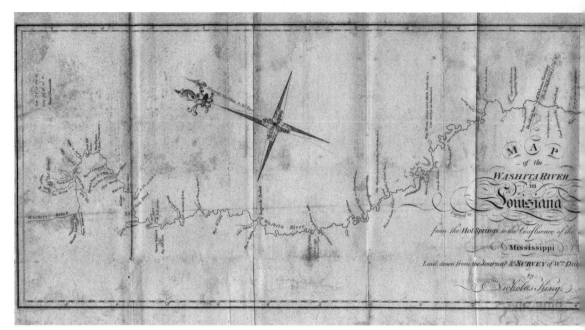

FIGURE 22. *Map of the Washita river in Louisiana from the Hot Springs to the confluence of the Red River with the Mississippi laid down from the Journal & survey of Wm. Dunbar in the year 1804,* by Nicholas King, published by R. Phillips, London, 1806. (American Memory Collection, Library of Congress)

Europe I had purchased every thing I could lay my hands on which related to any part of America, and particularly had a pretty full collection of the English, French & Spanish authors on the subject of Louisiana. The information I got from these was entirely satisfactory, and I threw it into a shape which would easily take the form of a Memorial. I now inclose you a copy of it. . . .

. . . Congress will probably authorise me to explore the greater waters on the Western side of the Missisipi, to their sources. In this case I should propose to send one party up the Panis river to it's source, thence along the highlands to the source of the Padoucas river, and down it to it's mouth. Another party up the Arcansa to it's source, thence along the highlands to the source of the Red river, & down that to it's moth, giving the whole course of both parties corrected by astronomical observations. These several

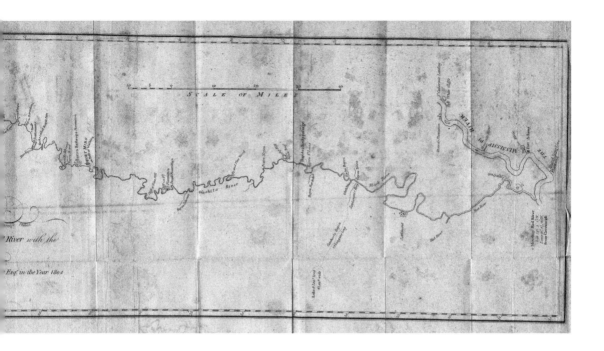

surveys will enable us to prepare a map of Louisiana, which in it's contour and main waters will be perfectly correct, & will give us a skeleton to be filled up with details hereafter. For what lies North of the Missouri we suppose British industry will furnish that. As you live so near to the point of departure of the lowest expedition, and possess and can acquire so much better the information which may direct that to the best advantage, I have thought if congress should authorise the enterprise to propose to you the unprofitable trouble of directing it. The party would consist of 10 or 12 picked souldiers, volunteers with an officer, under the guidance of one or two persons qualified to survey & correct by observations of latitude & longitude the latter lunar, and as well informed as we can get them in the departments of botany, natural history & mineralogy . . . Instructions similar to those of Capt. Lewis would

FIGURE 23.
Carte Generale Du Roy-
aume De La Nouvelle
Espagne depuis le
Parallele de 16¼ jusqu'au
Parallele de 38¼ (Lati-
tude Nord). Dressee
Sur des Observations
Astronomiques et sur
l'ensemble des Materiaux
qui existoient a Mexico,
au commencement
de l'annee 1804,
by Alexander von
Humboldt. Jefferson
had seen this map prior
to its 1809 publication
by F. Schoell in Paris.
(David Rumsey Map
Collection)

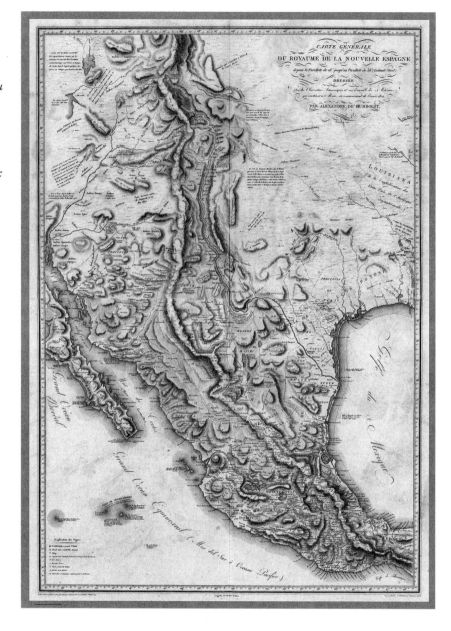

go from here to be added to by what should occur to yourself, and you would be the center from the communications from the party to the government. Still this is a matter of speculation only, as Congress are hurrying over their business for adjournment, and may leave this article of it unfinished. In that case what I have said will be as if I had not said it.[35]

Nicholas King, the talented city surveyor and architect, was directed to produce a map of the expedition, resulting in the 1806 publication of his *Map of the Washita river in Louisiana from the Hot Springs to the confluence of the Red River with the Mississippi* (fig. 22).[36] That Jefferson carefully reviewed the reports of the Dunbar-Hunter expedition, which preceded those of Lewis and Clark, is apparent in his February 1806 *Message from the President of the United States, Communicating Discoveries Made in Exploring the Missouri, Red River, and Washita, by Captains Lewis and Clark, Doctor Sibley, and Mr. Dunbar.*[37]

Planning for the 1806 Freeman-Custis expedition, the so-called "Grand Excursion" to the southwestern portions of the Louisiana Purchase, commenced shortly after Lewis and Clark began their journey. On 14 April 1804, Jefferson's instructions—bearing no slight resemblance to those for Lewis and Clark—to a young surveyor and engineer named Thomas Freeman stated:

> The government of the U.S. being desirous of informing itself to the extent of the Country lately ceded to them under the name of Louisiana to have the same with its principal rivers geographically delineated, you are appointed to explore for these purposes the interesting portion of it which lies on the Arkansas and Red Rivers, from their confluence with the Mississippi to the remotest source of the main streams of each and the high lands connecting the same and forming a part of the boundary of the Province.
> . . . From Natchez you are to proceed to ascend the Red river taking observations of longitude and latitude at its mouth, at all remarkable points in its course & especially at the mouths of rivers, at rapids, islands and other places & objects distinguished by such natural marks and characters of a durable kind as that they may with certainty be recognized thereafter. the courses of the rivers between these points of observation may be supplied by the compass the log line and by time corrected by the observations

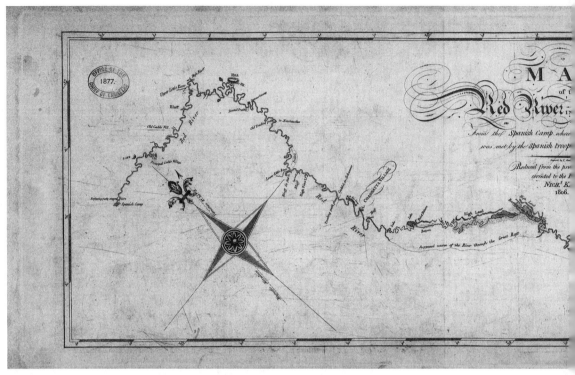

FIGURE 24. *Map of the Red River in Louisiana from the Spanish camp where the exploring party of the U.S. was met by the Spanish troops to where it enters the Mississippi, reduced from the protracted courses and corrected to the latitude,* by Nicholas King, published in Philadelphia, 1806. (American Memory Collection, Library of Congress)

themselves, the variations of the Compass too in different places are to be noted.[38]

Jefferson had substantial cartographic evidence, largely based on Alexander von Humboldt's as yet unpublished map "Carte Generale Du Royaume De La Nouvelle Espagne" (fig. 23), that the Red River would be the best route west to the region of New Mexico.[39] Unfortunately, due to a forceful and largely unanticipated resistance by the Spanish military, the Freeman-Custis expedition lasted a mere four months, and covered only half the river's course.[40] As with the Dunbar-Hunter expedition, Nicholas King was responsible for drafting a map summarizing the extent of the journey, with his 1806 *Map of the Red River in Loui-*

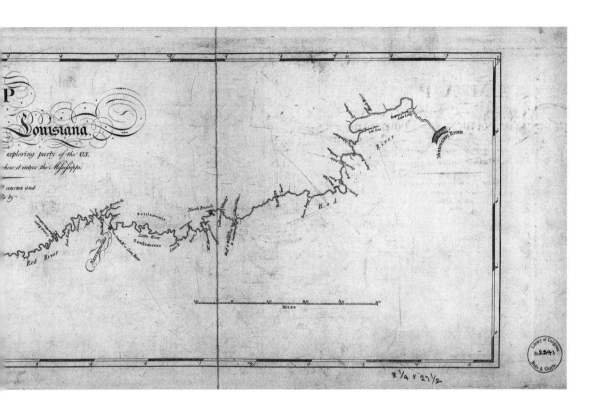

8 ¼ x 27 ½

siana from the Spanish camp where the exploring party of the U.S. was met by the Spanish troops to where it enters the Mississippi (fig. 24) the result.[41]

Thomas Jefferson was involved in planning these various expeditions for nearly two and one half decades, from his days as a congressional delegate through his presidency. After his administration ended, he was no longer closely involved in the planning of westward missions, although he still offered advice and commentary about various issues surrounding future westward expansion.

5

A GEOGRAPHY
OF LETTERS

❊ ❊ ❊
❊ ❊
❊

Jefferson was a late but prolific participant in the centuries-old, transatlantic Republic of Letters.[1] The output of this scholarly group of correspondents spanned the Renaissance through the European Enlightenment. The geographical range of Jefferson's correspondents was remarkable. Equally impressive and important were his wide-ranging references to geographic and cartographic information, including such related fields of discussion as agriculture, astronomy, exploration, meteorology, natural history, and politics.

On 30 July 1795, Christoph Daniel Ebeling, a prominent German scholar of America, geographer, and professor and teacher of Alexander von Humboldt, sent a letter introducing himself to Thomas Jefferson:

> Your worthy Country men Mr. J. Belknap and president Stiles of Yale College have exhorted me, to beg Your kind advice in an arduous task I have undertaken. I begun to publish a general History, Geography and Topographical description of America, whereto I have collected Materials as far as my situation would admit, since about twenty Years . . . My Book is on a far more larger plan than Mr. Morse's. Two Volumes are published containing only New England inclusive Vermont, and New York. I should have the honour to send You a Copy if I knew that you read our language, but as a french translation is now preparing with large additions and corrections, I shall defer till this appears, wishing to offer You a less defective production. The third Volume of the German Work is now printing and will comprehend N. Jersey, Pensylvania, Delaware and Maryland.
>
> The fourth is intended to complete the Work. As it will contain Virginia it would be impardonable, if I would not make use of

Your excellent Notes of Virginia. We have allready a German Abridgment thereof published by Professor Sprengel at Halle, and very well made, but rather to short. You will kindly allow that I may avail myself of Your instructive Work, quoting it allways with gratefull acknowledgment of my debt to You. I have the London edition of 1787.[2]

Ebeling's plans to use the *Notes on the State of Virginia* as a source of information speaks to the contemporary influence and quality of Jefferson's work. Ebeling goes on to outline his plan for the book, and comments:

I must end my long and egoistical Letter, for I fear I have tired your patience. Was it not for my ardent desire to promote human happiness in my country, by a faithfull picture of Your constitutions, Laws and Government, I should not have entered into such detail of my plan. I wish it may be honoured by Your approbation, and what is even more welcome to me, by Your remarks on its defects.

Jefferson wrote more than sixteen thousand letters and documents. This may not seem like much relative to the volumes of digital communications sent by modern teenagers,[3] but considering his range of scholarly and personal interests, and in light of the rigors of writing, it is an astounding output.[4] It is no surprise that a significant number of his communications reflected his geographical interests and knowledge, particularly given the importance of land and landscape to the early republic.[5] His correspondents in this exchange of geographical information included architects, cartographers, geographers, entrepreneurs, explorers, and various government officials and scientists.

Jefferson's writings regarding geographical concerns began early and necessarily paralleled the various phases of his career as a lawyer, member of the Virginia House of Burgesses, governor of Virginia, member of the Continental Congress, minister to France, secretary of state, vice president, president (and expedition planner), and elder statesman. Some of his geographically grounded projects spanned decades, including his ongoing building and renovation of Monticello, and his two-and-a-half-decade involvement with the planning and development of the federal city in Washington, D.C.

Jefferson's communications dealing with geographic or cartographic subjects are admittedly extensive, so my intent here is to provide a sampling—admittedly subjective—of some of that correspondence, in order to foreground the range of subjects and concerns addressed therein. In a 1769 letter to Virginia farmer and future politician Alexander White, written during Jefferson's tenure in the Virginia House of Burgesses, he notes:

> As to the larger tract of 400 acres which Harrison has entered, Mrs. Wood and James, as I understand you, will be passive: and opposition can only come from Harrison who may interplead to support his own right. Here then it will be necessary to prove the prior entry and survey made by Colo. Wood, by a copy of the entry under the surveior's hand and also of the platt if it is to be had.[6]

In that same year, in an invoice from bookseller Perkins, Buchanan and Brown, there is an entry for William Petty's landmark work, the *Survey of Ireland*.[7]

During his years as a member of the Continental Congress and through the course of the Revolution, Jefferson was involved—as were many others—with numerous geographical concerns, both military and political. In October of 1780, while governor of Virginia, he wrote to General Horatio Gates:

> Colo. Senf arrived here the Evening before the last. He was employed yesterday and to-day in copying some actual and accurate Surveys which we had made of the Country round about Portsmouth, as far as Cape Henry to the Eastward, Nansemond River to the Westward, the Dismal Swamp to the Southward, and Northwardly, the line of Country from Portsmouth by Hampton and York to Williamsburg and including the Vicinities of these three last posts. This will leave him nothing to do but to take drawings of particular places and the Soundings of such Waters as he thinks material.[8]

In a letter of 8 March 1781 to the Marquis de Lafayette, Jefferson observed:

> Scows I am afraid cannot be used for the Transportation of your Cannon on the wide Waters where your Operations will be

carried on. We shall endeavour to procure other vessels the best we can. The total Destruction of our Trade by the Enemy has put it out of our Power to make any great Collection of Boats. Some armed vessels of public and some of private property are held in readiness to cooperate, but as they are in James River they cannot venture down 'til the Command of the Water is again taken from the Enemy. Baron Steuben is provided with the most accurate drawings we have of the vicinities of Portsmouth: they are from actual Survey of the Land and as to information of the navigation the most authentick will be obtained from the pilots in that neighbourhood, ten of the best of which are provided.[9]

About a week later, in another letter to Lafayette, he noted:

I have the pleasure to inclose you herewith a small map of the vicinities of Williamsburg, York, Hampton and Portsmouth done on a scale of 5 miles to the inch which may serve for Pocket Purposes, and a larger one of the vicinities of Portsmouth on a scale of a mile to the inch which may be resorted to where greater accuracy is requisite. They are both from actual surveys and are the best in our power to provide for you. The larger one is a Copy of original draughts, the smaller is very carefully reduced from them.[10]

Another series of significant letters, beginning in late 1780 and eventually culminating in the publication of Jefferson's *Notes on the State of Virginia,* comprised his communications with François Marbois, then secretary to Anne-César, Chevalier de la Luzerne, the French minister to the fledgling United States of America. As discussed in chapter 2, Jefferson's detailed responses to Marbois's twenty-two queries, which had been sent to all colonial governors, became the basis of Jefferson's only published book.[11]

Thomas Hutchins is well known to historians of eighteenth-century cartography. A New Jersey native, he became the first and only "geographer of the United States" in 1781. Just prior to that appointment, he was a military surveyor and mapmaker for the Continental Army. In January of 1784, before he was posted to Paris as commissioner to France, Jefferson wrote to Hutchins, querying him about a possible error in his 1778 publication, *A Topographical Description of Virginia, Pennsylvania, Maryland, and North Carolina.* Jefferson's concerns were likely related to his interests in the future settlement of the Northwest Territory (the lands northwest of the Ohio River, which included much of the southwestern region surrounding the Great Lakes):

I have been recurring to your pamphlet (which I borrowed for that purpose) for the times at which the inundations begin and end in the Missouri, Missisipi, Illinois, Ohio, Wabache, but I do not find it mentioned there. Will you be so kind as to give me as accurate an account of these times as you can? Does the Tanissee overflow periodically? I suppose not. Will you give me leave to correct an error in your pamphlet page 13. where you say that the country extending from Fort Pitt to the Missisipi and on both sides watered by the Ohio and it's branches contains at least a million of square miles. I think the Ohio in all it's parts and branches cannot water more than the fourth of that. Count the degrees in your map into which it pushes it's branches. You will find them not quite 80, but suppose them made 80 by the branch of the Tanissee which heads in S. Carola. A degree in the middle of this space would contain about 3000, or 3100 square miles and of course 80 would contain about 250,000. I think the whole United states reduced to a square would not be more than one of 900 miles each way and of course that the whole U.S. do not contain a million of square miles. Excuse my freedom. I think this an error in your pamphlet and would wish to know from you whether I see it wrong. I am with much esteem Sir Your most obedt. Servt.[12]

Another of Jefferson's communications regarding the Northwest Territory was a lengthy and geographically detailed note to future president James Madison, then a member of the Virginia House of Delegates, dated 20 February 1784:

We have received the act of our assembly ceding the lands North of Ohio and are about executing a deed for it. I think the territory will be laid out by passing a meridian through the Western cape of the Mouth of the Gr. Kanhaway from the Ohio to L. Erie, and another through the rapids of Ohio from the same river to Michigan and crossing these by the parallels of latitude 37°.39°.41°. &c. allowing to each state an extent of 2°. from N. to South. On the Eastern side of the meridian of Kanhaway will still be one new state, to wit, the territory lying between that meridian, Pennsylva., the Ohio and L. Erie. We hope N. Carola. will cede all beyond the same meridian of Kanhaway, and Virginia also. For god's sake push this at the next session of assembly. We have transmitted a copy of a petition from the people of Kentucky to Congress praying to be separated from Virginia. Congress took no notice of it. We sent the copy to the Governor desiring it to be laid before the assembly. Our view was to bring on the question. It is for the interest of Virginia to cede so far immediately; because the people beyond that will separate themselves, because they will be joined by all our settlements beyond the Alleghaney if they are the first movers. Whereas if we draw the line those at Kentucky having their end will not interest themselves for the people of Indiana, Greenbriar &c. who will of course be left to our management, and I can with certainty almost say that Congress would approve of the meridian of the mouth of Kanhaway and consider it as the ultimate point to be desired from Virginia. I form this opinion from conversation with many members. Should we not be the first movers, and the Indianians and Kentuckians take themselves off and claim to the Alleghaney I am afraid Congress would secretly wish them well. Virginia is extremely interested to retain to that meridian: 1. Because the Gr. Kanhaway runs from North to South across our whole country forming by it's waters a belt of fine land, which will be thickly seated and will form a strong barrier for us. 2. Because the country for 180 miles beyond that is an absolute desart, barren and mountainous which can never be inhabited, and will therefore be a fine separation between us and the next state. 3. Because the government of Virginia is more convenient to the people on all the upper parts of Kanhaway than any other which will be laid out. 4. Because our lead mines are in that country. 5. Because the Kanhaway is capable of being made navigable, and therefore gives entrance into the Western waters to every part of our latitude. 6. Because it is not now navigable and can only be made so by expensive works, which require that we should own the soil on both sides. 7. Because the Ohio, and it's branches which head up against the Patowmac affords the shortest water communication by 500. miles of any which can ever be got between the Western waters and Atlantic, and of course promises us almost a monopoly of the Western and Indian trade. I think the opening this navigation is an object on which no time is to be lost. Pennsylva. is attending to the Western commerce. She has had surveys made of the river Susquehanna and of the grounds thro' which a canal must pass to go directly to Philadelphia. It is reported practicable at an expence of £200,000 and they have determined to open it. What an example this is! If we do not push this matter immediately they will be beforehand with us and get possession of the commerce. And it is difficult to turn it from a channel in which it is once established. Could not our assembly be induced to lay a particular tax which should bring in 5. or 10,000£ a year to be applied till the navigation of the Ohio and Patowmac is opened, then James river and so on through the whole successively. . . . The portage between Yohogania and the N. branch of Patowmac is of 40 or 50 miles. Cheat river is navigable far up. It's head is within 10 miles of the head of the North branch of Patowmac and I am informed offers the shortest and best portage.[13]

A letter from Madison to Jefferson, dated 9 January 1785, considers (among other things) "An act for opening and extending the navigation of Potowmac river." As Madison notes, several related resolutions were discussed or passed, including:

By another Resolution of this State, persons are to be forthwith appointed by the Executive to survey the upper parts of Jas. [James] river, the country thro' which a road must pass to the avigable waters of New River, and these waters down to the Ohio. I am told by a member of the Assembly who seems to be well acquainted both with the intermediate ground and with the Western waters in question, that a road of 25 or 30 miles in length will link these waters with Js. [James] river and will strike a branch of the former which yields a fine navigation, and falls into the main stream of the Kenhawha below the only obstructions lying in this river down to the Ohio. If these be facts James River will have a great superiority over Potowmac, the road from which to Cheat river is indeed computed by Genl. Washington at 20 miles only: but he thinks the expence of making the latter navigable will require a continuation of the road to Monongalia, which will lengthen it to 40 miles. The road to Yohogania is computed by the General at 30 miles.[14]

George Rogers Clark, Revolutionary War general and older brother of William Clark, had ongoing correspondence with Jefferson for more than a decade, often related to matters of major contemporary geopolitical concern. In a letter dated 29 January 1780, Jefferson wrote to Clark to discuss building a fort at the mouth of the Ohio River, land purchases from the Cherokee Nation, and a potential layout for future village plots:

I am glad the proposition of establishing a post at or near the mouth of Ohio is likely to answer as well in practice as to us, who judged on theory only, it seemed likely to do. I have therefore written to Messrs. Walker and Smith . . . to take observations of the latitudes thereabouts that we may proceed on the surest grounds. . . . I expect the description of the Cliffs &c will be so minute as that when you see them you will know them in the plat and of course know their latitude. The choice of the ground for your fort must be left to yourself. It should be as near the mouth of Ohio as can be found fit for fortification and within our own lines. Some attention will be proper also to the circumjacent grounds as it will probably become a Town of importance. The nature of the defensive works and their extent you will accommodate to your force. I would reccommend your attention to the wood of which you make your stockades, that it be of the most lasting kind. From the best information I have had, I take for granted that our line will pass below the mouth of Ohio. Our purchases of the Cherokees hitherto have not extended Southward or Westward of the Tanissee. Of course the little tract of country between the Missisipi, Ohio, Tanissee and Carolina line (in which your fort will be) is still to be purchased from them before you can begin your works. . . . If the new fort should fall within this territory and it can be purchased we may grant lands to settlers who will fix round about the fort, provided the Assembly should approve of it, as from its reasonableness I think they will. The manner in which the lots of land are laid off about the french villages I have thought very wise and worthy of imitation.[15]

Jefferson was always looking for new information about the western regions of the continent, as exemplified by another letter to Clark in November 1782:

> You will perhaps hear of my being gone to Europe, but my trip there will be short. I mention this lest you should hesitate in forwarding any curiosities for me. Any observations of your own on the subject of the big bones or their history, or on any thing else in the Western country, will come acceptably to me, because I know you see the works of nature in the great, and not merely in detail. Descriptions of animals, vegetables, minerals, or other curious things, notes as to the Indians, information of the country between the Missisipi and waters of the South sea &c. &c. will strike your mind as worthy being communicated. I wish you had more time to pay attention to them.[16]

In December of 1783, prompted by his fears of future British expeditions with the hidden intent of colonization, Jefferson again wrote to General Clark about the possibility of leading an expedition into lands west of the Mississippi River. There was short, added mention about evolving plans for the location of the future federal city:

> I find they have subscribed a very large sum of money in England for exploring the country from the Missisipi to California. They pretend it is only to promote knolege. I am afraid they have thoughts of colonising into that quarter. Some of us have been talking here in a feeble way of making the attempt to search that country. But I doubt whether we have enough of that kind of spirit to raise the money. How would you like to lead such a party? Tho I am afraid our prospect is not worth asking the question. The definitive treaty of peace is at length arrived. It is not altered from the preliminaries. The cession of the territory West of Ohio to the United states has been at length accepted by Congress with some small alterations of the conditions. We are in daily expectation of receiving it with the final approbation of Virginia. Congress have been lately agitated by questions where they should fix their residence. They first resolved on Trentown. The Southern states however contrived to get a vote that they would give half their time to Georgetown at the Falls of Patowmac.[17]

Although Clark declined to lead an expedition, he continued his correspondence with Jefferson while endorsing the future prospect (a point discussed at length in chapter 4).[18]

David Rittenhouse was an American scientific polymath (astronomer, mathematician, surveyor, and clockmaker) and a longtime friend of and scientific adviser to Jefferson. In a letter dated 14 April 1787, Rittenhouse wrote Jefferson about various geographical and cartographical matters pertaining to publications of the American Philosophical Society:

> We have abundance of projectors and pretendors to new Discoveries, and many applications to the Legislature for exclusive priviledges, some of them ridiculous enough. The selfmoving Boat, the Steam Boat, the Mechanical Miller, the improved Ring Dial for finding the Variations of the Needle. The Surveying Compass to serve 20 other purposes, And a project for finding the Longitude by the Variation of the Magnetical Needle. Of this I shall give you a more particular Account. The Authors first scheme was this. He supposes two invisible Globes, appendages of the Earth, to Govern the Needle and likewise greatly to influence the Tides, one having 70 or 80 Degrees North Declination and the other almost as much South, and he has Assigned the periods of their revolutions. But being told that his Globes would infallibly fall to the Earth unless Supported by an Iron Spike or something of that nature, he has discharged them and contented himself with assigning two points, one near each pole. Thro' the Northern one, he says, pass all the Magnetical Meridians in the Northern Hemisphere, and thro' the other all those of the Southern Hemisphere. He has determined the present situation and periodical revolution of the North point with great precission, of the other he speaks more doubtfully. In a plausible publication he proposes on these principles to find the Longitude Generally and thinks himself intitled to a public reward.[19]

Shortly following this note, Jefferson received a detailed, length discussion about longitude from John Churchman, a notable Pennsylvania surveyor:

The Memorial of John Churchman respectfully represents that the Variation of the Compass and its hitherto imagined uncertain Laws have long engaged the attention of Philosophers And Mathematicians. Why it should move at one Time slow, at another Time quick, now become stationary and then retrograde, has puzzled the Enquirer, and although these varieties have been continually Subjects of observation, Yet I have never heard that any Regular System hath hitherto been published to account for or foretel upon any rational plan, what will be the future Movements of this wonderful Phenomenon, the Magnetic Influence. Whether My attempts to reconcile all these Difficulties and of consequence to build on them a certain System of Longitude will prove true or false must be left to the world to judge.

From a variety of observations, Reflections and Deductions, the following Conclusions are assumed.

- 1st. That the Magnetic Needle hath a Direction to two Points at certain Distances, one from the North, the other from the South Pole of the Earth.
- 2ly. That these Points, to which it hath a Direction are properly called Magnetic Poles.
- 3ly. That the Magnetic Poles perform Revolutions in certain given Times from West to East.
- 4ly. That by a Variety of Deductions, and by laying down Many observations of the variation of the Magnetic Needle, one of these Poles is found to be at a certain Distance from the North Pole of the Earth, which for distinction May be called the North Magnetic Pole.
- 5ly. That the orbit in which the South Magnetic Pole moves, is larger than the Northern orbit.
- 6ly. That the angle between a Meridian of the Earth and the Magnetic Meridian is the Variation of the Compass.
- 7ly. That the Northern Magnetic Pole in 1779 was in Latitude 76.°4′ and Longitude 85.°12′ west from London and its period of Revolution is 463 years 344 days.
- 8ly. That the Situation of the Southern Magnetic Pole for want of a sufficient Number of observations, I have not yet so accurately determined, but in the Year 1777 I calculate it to

have been in 72 degrees South Latitude and 140 degrees East Longitude from London or Greenwich.

That from hence the Longitude of either Pole is easily determined, and I have formed a Sett of Tables of their Annual Situations from the Year 1657 (when a Line of no variation passed over London) to the Year 1888, when a Line of no Variation will again pass the same Place.

That having the Latitude of the Magnetic Poles and by ascertaining the Longitude of the same from the Tables for any given Time, we are able to determine the Longitude of any Place with the greatest Precision from a combined observation of the Latitude of the Place and the Variation of the Magnetic Needle.

It may be necessary to observe that a Magnetic Meridian for any part of this Globe is a circle drawn through the two Magnetic Poles and the place of observation. If the Magnetic Poles were diametrically opposite to each other, the Line of no Variation would coincide with the Meridian of the Earth, and all the Magnetic Meridians would of consequence be great Circles; but though this is not the case, the Longitude is determined by a Method full as simple as if they were great Circles; that the Magnetic Meridians meet in the two Magnetic Poles, and that these Poles are in certain parts of their orbits in certain Times. There is sufficient Proof, by laying down on a Globe the observations of the Variation Made by the late celebrated Cap. Cook in his last Voyage round the world as well as those made by other able Navigators.[20]

Pierre Charles L'Enfant, the iconic French-born architect and civil engineer who immigrated to America in 1777, was one of Jefferson's better-known correspondents. In 1791, President Washington appointed L'Enfant to design plans for the new federal city on the banks of the Potomac River.[21] Jefferson, then serving as the first secretary of state of the new republic, was the primary conduit for communication with L'Enfant, and they exchanged roughly a dozen letters before L'Enfant's dismissal in February of 1792. In early March of 1791, Jefferson wrote:

You are desired to proceed to George town where you will find Mr. Ellicot employed in making a survey and map of the federal territory. The special object of asking your aid is to have drawings of the particular grounds most likely to be approved for the site of the federal town and buildings. You will therefore be pleased to begin on the Eastern branch, and proceed from thence upwards, laying down the hills, vallies, morasses, and waters between that, the Patowmac, the Tyber, and the road leading from George town to the Eastern branch, and connecting the whole with certain fixed points of the map Mr. Ellicot is preparing. Some idea of the height of the hills above the base on which they stand would be desireable. For necessary assistance and expences be pleased to apply to the Mayor of George town who is written to on this subject. I will beg the favour of you to mark to me your progress about twice a week, by letter, say every Wednesday and Saturday evening, that I may be able in proper time to draw your attention to some other objects which I have not at this moment sufficient information to define.[22]

As is evident from L'Enfant's response, dated 11 March 1791, he had difficulty mastering the nuances of the English language:

No part of the ground betwen the eastern branch and george town can be say to be of a commanding nature. On the contrary it appear at first sight as being closely surrounded—however in advancing toward the easterne branch these heights seem to sink as the waves of a tempestuous sea and when considering the intended city on that grand Scale on which it ought to be planed it will appear that the only height which would unavoidably batter in it, a small town may easily be comprehended in the limit and be of such a one as rendered by a proper menagement in the appropriation of the building that may be there erected a mean of protection and of security.[23]

To this, Jefferson promptly responded:

Your favor of the 11. inst. has been duly recieved. Between the date of that and your reciept of the present, it is probable that the most important parts of the ground towards the Eastern branch will have been delineated. However, whether they are or not, as the President will go on within two or three days, and would wish to have under his eye, when at Georgetown, a drawing also of the principal lineaments of the ground between Rock creek and the Tyber, you are desired, immediately on the reciept of this, to commence the survey of that part, beginning at the river, and proceeding towards the parts back of that till his arrival. If the meanders of these two creeks and of the river between them should not have been already laid down either by yourself or Mr. Ellicot, it is desired that Mr. Ellicot should immediately do this while you shall be employed on the interior ground, in order that the work may be as much advanced as possible on the arrival of the President, and that you will be so good as to notify this to Mr. Ellicot. I am with great esteem Sir Your most obedt. humble servt.

Th: Jefferson

P.S. There are certainly considerable advantages on the Eastern branch: but there are very strong reasons also in favor of the position between Rock creek and Tyber independant of the face of the ground. It is the desire that the public mind should be in equilibrio between these two places till the President arrives, and we shall be obliged to you to endeavor to poise their expectations.[24]

In a series of subsequent letters, Jefferson sends L'Enfant a number of his town plans of European cities, and a suggestion as to the layout of a proposed engraved map of the new federal city:

A person applied to me the other day on the subject of engraving a Map of the Federal territory. I observed to him that if yourself or Mr. Ellicot chose to have this done, you would have the best right to it. Do either of you intend this? If you do I would suggest to you the idea of doing it on a square sheet to hang corner upwards thus [Here Jefferson inserted a small sketch] The outlines being N.W. N.E. S.E. and S.W. the meridians will be vertical as they ought to be; the streets of the city will be horizontal and vertical, and near the center; the Patowmac and Eastern branch will be nearly so also; there will be no waste in the square sheet of paper.[25]

By early 1792, it was apparent that things were not going well, as indicated in a lengthy letter from Jefferson dated 26 February, followed by a letter a day later terminating L'Enfant's services.

Andrew Ellicott, the highly skilled surveyor and native Pennsylvanian who would one day teach surveying methods to Meriwether Lewis, had been in conflict with L'Enfant over his plans for the federal city.[26] Ellicott continued his survey work after L'Enfant's departure, and it was actually Ellicott's revised plan, engraved and printed by Thackera and Vallance in March of 1792, that is often identified as the first "official" plan of Washington, D.C. Jefferson's communications with Ellicott continued into his first presidential term.

In conjunction with those early surveys of the areas planned for Washington, D.C., Jefferson wrote Ellicott on 2 February 1791:

> You are desired to proceed by the first stage to the Federal territory on the Potomac, for the purpose of making a survey of it. The first object will be to run the two first lines mentioned in the enclosed proclamation to wit:—the S.W. line 160 poles and the S.E. line to Hunting creek or should it not strike Hunting creek as has been suggested then to the river. These two lines must be run with all the accuracy of which your art is susceptible as they are to fix the begining either on Hunting creek or the river. If the second line should strike the river instead of the creek take and lay down the bearing and distance of the nearest part of the creek and also of any of its waters if any of them should be nearer than the creek itself; so also should either of these two lines cross any water of Hunting creek let it be noted. The termination of the Second line being accurately fixed, either on the creek or river, proceed to run from that as a beginning the four lines of experiment directed in the proclamation. This is intended as the first rough essay to furnish data for the last accurate survey.[27]

In April of 1801, Ellicott wrote Jefferson regarding several geographically related subjects, including astronomical remarks pertaining to the determination of longitude:

> I have accompanied this by a few sheets of my observations, they contain an account of the work on the boundary as far as to Pearl, or half-way river. The manner of describing the prime vertical as mentioned at the beginning of the line, I have not found noticed by any writer, but should think it too obvious to be new.—I am sorry the plate containing the references is not yet engraved.—
>
> Whilst I was engaged in the City of Washington some years ago I made a number of observations to determine its longitude, but all of them with some papers relative to the plan of the City were lost, when the office was pillaged: But fortunately two very important

observations had been communicated to our late worthy friend Mr. Rittenhouse, and published in the 4th. volume of the Transactions of our Society.—The first is on an annular eclipse of the Sun, and the second an occultation of . . . Aldebaran by the moon.— Observations of this kind answer very well for the determination of the longitude, but the calculations are critical, and labourious, owing to the moon's parallax in altitude, latitude, and longitude, and therefore not in common use:—However for want of other materials, and having little to do besides correcting the press, I have gone thro' the calculations.—

The observation on the eclipse stands as below . . .

The observation on the eclipse was made about 10″ west from where the occultation was observed, which when deducted from the eclipse, the results will stand as below for the meridian of the Capitol . . .

From which it appears, (in the language Americans ought to use), that Greenwich is 5h 7′ 44.4? or 76° 56′ 6? east from the City of Washington.—

I have been long wanting our longitudes to be reckoned, or counted, from our own Capitol, and not from a place within another country; and for this purpose calculated, and published an Almanac with the sun's declination, eclipses of ♃ trs. Satellites &c. adapted to the meridian of the City of Washington, which I had estimated at 5h 8′ west from Greenwich, but the plan fell thro when I left the City.—

We appear yet to be connected to Great Britain by a number of small ligaments, which tho apparently unimportant, are never-theless a drawback upon that absolute independence we ought as a nation to maintain.—It would be very well when the longitude of the City of Washington is more accurately settled by a sufficient course of observations . . . to have an American gazetteer published, in which the longitudes should be reckoned east, and west from the Capitol.[28]

On 6 March 1803, Ellicott wrote to Jefferson indicating his willing-ness to train Meriwether Lewis in surveying techniques, in preparation for the landmark expedition:

Your agreeable favour of the 26th Ult. has been duly received, and the contents noted. I shall be very happy to see Captn. Lewis, and will with pleasure give him all the information, and instruction, in my power. The necessary apparatus for his intended, and very interesting expedition, you will find mentioned in the last paragraph of the 42d page of my printed observations made in our southern country, a copy of which I left with you. But exclusive of the watch, I would recommend one of Arnolds chronometers, (if it could be had,) for reasons which I will fully explain to Mr. Lewis.

Mr. Lewis's first object must be, to acquire a facility, and dexterity, in making the observations; which can only be attained by practice; in this he shall have all the assistance I can give him with aid of my apparatus. It is not to be expected that the calculations can be made till after his return, because the transportation of the books, and tables, necessary for that purpose, would be found inconvenient on such a journey. The observations on which Arrowsmith has constructed his map of the northern part of this country, were all calculated in England.[29]

Though the extensive communications to and from Jefferson regarding this expedition are too numerous to document here, they speak volumes of the president's interest in its progress and the wonders that the explorers encountered during the journey.[30]

Another of Jefferson's planned expeditions into various areas of the Louisiana Purchase, led by George Hunter and William Dunbar (and discussed in chapter 4), began to take shape with Jefferson's initial communication to Dunbar on 24 June 1799:

I have long imagined that if there exists at this day, any evidence of their descent from any nation of the old world, it will be found in their languages. it must require an immense tract of time indeed for two languages, originally the same, to recede from each other till all appearances of their common origin shall be lost. it is therefore interesting to make as copious a collection as possible of the languages of the Indian tribes inhabiting America. I have for some time been availing myself of such opportunities of doing this as have occurred to me. some others in this quarter have done the same; so that we are likely to make a tolerable collection of those on this side the Missisipi. beyond that river our means fail. it is therefore with great pleasure I have learnt that so advanced a post as the Natchez possesses a gentleman so well qualified as yourself to extend enquiries into the regions beyond that. a lover of science cannot want the zeal requisite to engage his aid in it's promotion. on this ground I have presumed to ask you to procure for us what, with convenience, you can procure in this way, from the country beyond your position. the Chickasaws & Choctaws are the most remote of those whom our enquiries have reached. and as it is material, for the purpose of comparison, that our enquiries should go to the same objects, I take the liberty of inclosing to you some blank copies of the vocabularies we have used & of asking the favor of you to procure them to be filled from such tribes beyond the Missisipi as are within our reach.[31]

Dunbar responded in early October 1799:

I am honored by the receipt of yours of 24 June last. It is highly gratifying to be invited by a person of your high reputation in the republic of letters to contribute in conducting philosophical researches in this and the neighboring country—Constant occupation as a planter since my residence in this country has somewhat disqualified me for scientific pursuits—.&c xxx But shall take pleasure in pursuing such objects of enquiry as you may point out as worthy of the attention of your Society—

I keep a regular diary of the weather and the rise and fall of the Thermometer and Barometer the quantity of rain that falls with the direction & Strength of the wind &c of which I will forward you copies— . . . xx.

The natural history of this country so far as I have had an opportunity of visiting it will be found to vary very little from that of the same latitude in the Atlantic States: The forest trees are the same which generally grow from Virginia to Florida. The richest lands are covered with strong canes growing very close which excluding all other Vigetable subjects a few large trees excepted furnish no field for the Botanist—the open woods land and plains are more productive of variety but I believe little is to be found which has escaped the researches of the indefatigable deciples of Linæus.[32]

Their geographic and scientific correspondence continued—covering such subjects as meteorology, topography, and linguistic geography—as per Jefferson's letter dated 12 January 1801:

The papers addressed to me, I took the liberty of communicating to the Philosophical society. that on the language by signs is quite new. soon after recieving your meteorological diary, I recieved one of Quebec: and was struck with the comparison between −32. & +19 ¾ the lowest depressions of the thermometer at Quebec & the Natchez. I have often wondered that any human being should live in a cold country who can find room in a warm one. I have no doubt but that cold is the source of more sufferance to all animal nature than hunger, thirst, sickness & all the other pains of life & of death itself put together. I live in a temperate climate, and under circumstances which do not expose me often to cold. . . . what then must be the sum of that evil if we take in the vast proportion of men who are obliged to be out in all weather, by land & by sea; all the families of beasts, birds, reptiles, & even the vegetable kingdom? for that too has life, and where there is life there may be sensation.—I remark a rainbow of a great portion of the circle observed by you when on the line of demarcation. I live in a situation which has given me an opportunity of seeing more than the semicircle often. I am on a hill 500. f. perpendicular high. on the east side it breaks down abruptly to the base where a river passes through. a rainbow therefore about sunset plunges one of it's legs down to the river, 500. f. below the level of the eye on the top of the hill. I have twice seen bows formed by the moon. they were of the colour of the common circle round the moon, and were very near, being within a few paces of me in both instances.—I thank you for the little vocabularies of Bedaïs, Tankawis & Teghas. I have it much at heart to make as extensive a collection as possible of the Indian tongues. I have at present about 30. tolerably full, among which the number radically different, is truly wonderful. it is curious to consider how such handfuls of men, came by different languages, & how they have preserved them so distinct. I at first thought of reducing them all to one orthography. but I soon became sensible that this would occasion two sources of error instead of one. I therefore think it best to keep them in the form of orthography in which they were taken, only noting whether that were English, French, German or what.[33]

The notable French philosopher and historian Constantin-François de Chasseboeuf, Comte de Volney, was another regular Jeffersonian correspondent through the late eighteenth and early nineteenth centuries. Jefferson wrote to Volney about a number of matters, including weather and wind, on 8 January 1797:

I am sorry you have recieved so little information on the subject of our winds. I had once (before our revolution war) a project on the same subject. As I had then an extensive acquaintance over this state, I meant to have engaged some person in every county of it, giving them each a thermometer to observe that, and the winds twice a day for one year, to wit at sunrise and at 4. P.M. (the coldest and warmest point of the 24. hours) and to communicate their observations to me at the end of the year. I should then have selected the days in which it appeared that the winds blew to a center within the state, and have made a map of them, and seen how far they had analogy with the temperature of the air. I meant this to be merely a specimen to be communicated to the Philosopl. society at Philadelphia, in order to engage them, by means of their correspondents, to have the same thing done in every state, and through a series of years. By seising the days when the winds centered in any part of the United states, we might in time have come at some of the causes which determine the direction of the winds, which I suspect to be very various.[34]

Alexander von Humboldt, the German politician, explorer, geographer, and scientist often considered the father of modern geography, was a friend and correspondent of Jefferson's.[35] In one frequently quoted letter from early December 1813, Jefferson wrote to him about a number of their shared interests:

The livraison of your astronomical observations, and the 6th and 7th on the subject of New Spain, with the corresponding atlasses, are duly received, as had been the preceding cahiers. For these treasures of a learning so interesting to us, accept my sincere thanks. I think it most fortunate that your travels in those countries were so timed as to make them known to the world in the moment they were about to become actors on its stage. . . . The European nations constitute a separate division of the globe; their localities make them part of a distinct system; they have a set of interests of their own in which it is our business never to engage ourselves. America has a hemisphere to itself. . . .

That their Arrowsmith should have stolen your Map of Mexico, was in the piratical spirit of his country. But I should be sincerely sorry if our Pike has made an ungenerous use of your candid communications here; and the more so as he died in the arms of victory gained over the enemies of his country. Whatever he did was on a principle of enlarging knowledge . . .

You will find it inconceivable that Lewis's journey to the Pacific should not yet have appeared; nor is it in my power to tell you the reason. The measures taken by his surviving companion, Clarke, for the publication, have not answered our wishes in point of despatch. I think, however, from what I have heard, that the mere journal will be out within a few weeks in two volumes 8vo . . . The botanical and zoological discoveries of Lewis will probably experience greater delay, and become known to the world through other channels before that volume will be ready. The Atlas, I believe, waits on the leisure of the engraver.[36]

Bishop James Madison, a cousin of the future president, was another well-educated correspondent of Jefferson's.[37] In early March of 1798, Jefferson wrote to Madison about a number of related scientific concerns, including problems of measuring magnetic declination, the moons of Jupiter, and a new system of geography.[38] Madison promptly replied with respect to detailed experiments concerning magnetic declination.[39]

A letter from Jefferson to Bishop Madison in late December 1811 expands and develops their ongoing correspondence related to astronomy, geography, and cartography:

I thank you for mr Lambert's calculation on my observations of the late eclipse of the sun. I have been for some time rubbing up my Mathematics from the rust contracted by 50. years pursuits of a different kind, and thanks to the good foundation laid at College by my old master & friend Small, I am doing it with a delight & success beyond my expectation. I had observed the eclipse of Sep. 17. with a view to calculate from it myself the longitude of

Monticello; but other occupations had prevented it before my journey. the elaborate paper of mr Lambert shews me it would have been a more difficult undertaking than I had foreseen, & that probably I should have foundered in it. I have no telescope equal to the observation of the eclipses of Jupiter's satellites. but as soon as I can fit up a box to fix my instruments in, I propose to amuse myself with further essays to fix our longitude by the lunar observations, which have the advantages of multiplied repetitions & less laborious calculations. I have a fine theodolite & Equatorial both by Ramsden, a Hadley's circle of Borda, a fine meridian and horizon as you know. once ascertaining the dip of my horizon I can use the circle, as at sea, without an artificial horizon. do you think of ever giving us a second edition of your map? if you do I may be able to furnish you with some latitudes. I have a pocket sextant of miraculous accuracy, considering it's microscopic graduation with this I have ascertained the lat. of Poplar Forest, (say New London) by multiplied observations, & lately that of Willis's mountains by observations of my own, repeated by my grandson, whom I am carrying on in his different studies.[40]

In addition to such figures as Ebeling, Hutchins, and Bishop Madison, Jefferson also corresponded with John Melish, a highly skilled mapmaker and Philadelphia publisher, and a prominent figure in the early history of cartography in the United States. Melish was born in Scotland and immigrated to the United States in 1811.[41] On 18 January 1812, Melish wrote to Jefferson concerning his plans to publish what would become a landmark work of United States geography, *Travels in the United States of America in the Years 1806 & 1807, and 1809, 1810, & 1811*:

I have lately returned from a very extended Tour to the Western Country, and now intend to prepare my whole Travels for the Press, as you will see by the enclosed Prospectus, and Plan.—I have commenced procuring Subscribers here with considerable success, and intend soon to visit the Seat of government in prosecution of that object, when I will, perhaps, also go into Virginia. In the meantime it will [be] of considerable importance if You will permit me to add your name to the List of Subscribers, for one or more Copies; and it would be esteemed a very particular favour if you would condescend to give me any information regarding the chance of procuring Subscribers in Your State. The design of the work I submit to your judgement without Comment. I intend to have it also published in Britain, provided I can make arrangements to that effect; and my object is to render a service to the Inhabitants of both Countries.[42]

Jefferson did subscribe to the publication and was duly impressed with Melish's work:

I received duly your favor of December the 15th, and with it the copies of your map and travels, for which be pleased to accept my thanks. The book I have read with extreme satisfaction and information. As to the western States, particularly, it has greatly edified me: for of the actual condition of that interesting portion of our country, I had not an adequate idea. I feel myself now as familiar with it as with the condition of the maritime States. I had no conception that manufactures had made such progress there . . .

To return to the merits of your work: I consider it as so lively a picture of the real state of our country, that if I can possibly obtain opportunities of conveyance, I propose to send a copy to a friend in France, and another to one in Italy, who, I know, will translate and circulate it as an antidote to the misrepresentations of former travelers.[43]

Melish also sent the retired president a copy of his landmark *Map of the United States with the contiguous British & Spanish Possessions Compiled from the latest & best Authorities,* published in 1816. This work is often cited as the first cartographic foreshadowing of Manifest Destiny (a subject to which we will turn in the next chapter). Jefferson was again struck by the quality of Melish's work, and commented so at length:

Your favor of November 23d, after a very long passage, is received, and with it the map which you have been so kind as to send me, for which I return you many thanks. It is handsomely executed, and on a well-chosen scale; giving a luminous view of the comparative possessions of different powers in our America. It is on account of the value I set on it, that I will make some suggestions. By the charter of Louis XIV. all the country comprehending the waters which flow into the Mississippi, was made a part of Louisiana. Consequently its northern boundary was the summit of the highlands in which its northern waters rise. But by the Xth Art. of the Treaty of Utrecht, France and England agreed to. appoint commissioners to settle the boundary between their possessions in that quarter, and those commissioners settled it at the 49 th degree of latitude. See Hutchinson's Topographical Description of Louisiana, p. 7. This it was which induced the British Commissioners, in settling the boundary with us, to follow the northern water line to the Lake of the Woods, at the latitude of 49°, and then go off on that parallel. This, then, is the true northern boundary of Louisiana.

The western boundary of Louisiana is, rightfully, the Rio Bravo, (its main stream,) from its mouth to its source, and thence along the highlands and mountains dividing the waters of the Mississippi from those of the Pacific. The usurpations of Spain on the east side of that river, have induced geographers to suppose the Puerco or Salado to be the boundary. The line along the highlands stands on the charter of Louis XIV. that of the Rio Bravo, on the circumstance that, when La Salle took possession of the Bay of St. Bernard, Panuco was the nearest possession of Spain, and the Rio Bravo the natural half-way boundary between them.

On the waters of the Pacific, we can found no claim in right of Louisiana. If we claim that country at all, it must be on Astor's settlement near the mouth of the Columbia, and the principle of the jus gentium of America, that when a civilized nation takes possession of the mouth of a river in new country, that possession is considered as including all its waters.

The line of latitude of the southern source of the Multnomat might be claimed as appurtenant to Astoria. For its northern boundary, I believe an understanding has been come to between our government and Russia, which might be known from some of its members. I do not know it.

Although the irksomeness of writing, which you may perceive from the present letter, and its labor, oblige me now to withdraw from letter writing, yet the wish that your map should set to rights the ideas of our own countrymen, as well as foreign nations, as to our correct boundaries, has induced me to make these suggestions, that you may bestow on them whatever inquiry they may merit. I salute you with esteem and respect.[44]

This sampling of Jefferson's correspondence, and the varied points raised by his correspondents, provides a glimpse into his concerns, his capabilities, and his hopes for the fledgling nation. When considered in the context of other documents scattered throughout these pages, we begin to understand the diverse nature of his own epistolary republic, and to gain a deeper appreciation of Jefferson's ongoing use of and reliance on geographic and cartographic information.

6

FORESHADOWING
MANIFEST DESTINY

❋ ❋ ❋
❋ ❋
❋

J efferson can be tied to nearly every general discussion about the continental expansion of the early republic.[1] The notion of Manifest Destiny was popularized in the mid-nineteenth century, although the roots of the conflicted concept go back centuries. The extant literature is extensive, and a number of overviews are available.[2] In the pages that follow, I will briefly discuss five major antecedents of the concept, how they link to Jefferson's political career, and particularly how they relate to his knowledge and use of geography and cartography. These key progenitors are the Bible, the Right of Discovery, Natural Law, the Louisiana Purchase, and the Lewis and Clark expedition, each of which has been documented and dissected elsewhere. Here we consider the cartographic foreshadowing of Manifest Destiny, particularly as it pertains to Jefferson's interests and concerns.

I am not suggesting that Jefferson's intellectual views and assertions were unique in the eighteenth century: they were not. He was a prominent American representative of the intellectual milieu of the European Enlightenment.[3] He provides a nexus for discussion, particularly given his expansive intellectual pursuits, his prolonged and well-chronicled political career, and the extent of his own written record. Geopolitical concerns have always, particularly at the highest levels, been a force in the expanse of our national politics.

Myths of destiny are numerous, often tied to specific geographical regions and peoples.[4] In European North America, these began with the New World hopes and dreams of the French and Spanish.[5] In the United States, the iconic phrase "Manifest Destiny" is one such assertion, conceptually mixing such elements as the virtue of the American people and their governmental institutions, a redemptive mission to spread these institutions, and a destiny under God to perform this mission.[6]

The origin of the phrase is usually attributed to John L. O'Sullivan, editor of *The United States Magazine and Democratic Review,* who referred to it in the summer of 1845, in his support of the addition of Texas to the Union:

> Why, were other reasoning wanting, in favor of now elevating this question of the reception of Texas into the Union, out of the lower region of our past party dissensions, up to its proper level of a high and broad nationality, it surely is to be found, found abundantly, in the manner in which other nations have undertaken to intrude themselves into it, between us and the proper parties to the case, in a spirit of hostile interference against us, for the avowed object of thwarting our policy and hampering our power, limiting our greatness and checking the fulfillment of our manifest destiny to overspread the continent allotted by Providence for the free development of our yearly multiplying millions.[7]

This appearance notwithstanding, substantive evidence indicates that the historic phrase was penned by Jane McManus Storm Cazneau, writing under the pseudonym of Cora Montgomery, while she was employed as a staff writer by O'Sullivan.[8]

The initial expression of Manifest Destiny, although often imbued with messianic overtones, was grounded in geography. It was rooted in the expansive physical resources and perceived aesthetic values of the North American landscape.[9] The idea of Manifest Destiny was not simply tied to contemporary historical experience, but also to the physical nature of its spaces.[10] Messianic though it might be, the concept was rooted in land and landscape.

Thomas Jefferson has been linked to the ideas of Manifest Destiny on several levels,[11] and the formal phrase is prefigured in his writings. In a 1786 letter to Archibald Judge Stuart, a native Pennsylvanian who had settled his family in Virginia, Jefferson observed, "Our confederacy must be viewed as the nest from which all America, North & South is to be peopled."[12] In 1801, during his first inaugural address, he referred to "a rising nation, spread over a wide and fruitful land, traversing all the seas with the rich productions of their industry, engaged in commerce with nations who feel power and forget right, advancing rapidly to destinies beyond the reach of mortal eye."[13]

In an 1803 letter to John Breckinridge, patriarch of a prominent Virginia political family and future U.S. senator and attorney general, Jefferson asserted:

> When I view the Atlantic States, procuring for those on the Eastern waters of the Mississippi friendly instead of hostile neighbors on its Western waters, I do not view it as an Englishman would the procuring future blessings for the French nation, with whom he has no relations of blood or affection. The future inhabitants of the Atlantic & Mississippi States will be our sons. We leave them in distinct but bordering establishments. We think we see their happiness in their union, & we wish it.[14]

In May of 1812, Jefferson wrote to John Jacob Astor regarding the future development of the northwest fur trade and supporting the idea of a factory on the Columbia River, emphasizing that he considered "as a great public acquisition the commencement of a settlement on that point of the Western coast of America, unconnected with us but by the ties of blood and interest, and employing like us the rights of self government."[15] Alexander von Humboldt, recalling his 1804 visit with Jefferson in later years, reported that the president discussed "the project of a future division of the American continent into three great republics which were to include Mexico and the South American states which at that time belonged to the Spanish crown."[16] In 1813, Jefferson's oft-quoted letter to Humboldt further articulated his vision:

> America has a hemisphere to itself. It must have its separate system of interests, which must not be subordinated to those of Europe. . . . In fifty years more the United States alone will contain fifty millions of inhabitants, and fifty years are soon gone over. The peace of 1763 is within that period. I was then twenty years old, and of course remember well all the transactions of the war preceding it. And you will live to see the epoch now equally ahead of us; and the numbers which will then be spread over the other parts of the American hemisphere, catching long before that the principles of our portion of it, and concurring with us in the maintenance of the same system.[17]

There is substantive evidence of the biblical roots of Manifest Destiny, including the ideal of a promised land and a chosen people.[18] Biblical allusions were commonplace in western European, and hence colonial American, political discourse between the sixteenth and eighteenth centuries. An early assertion of a special destiny, a secularized "Holy Commonwealth" for North Americans can be found in the writings of the early Puritan settlers.[19]

Thomas Jefferson invokes the idea of a "chosen" people and place on several occasions. Writing to James Monroe in 1785, he exclaimed, "My God! How little do my countrymen know what precious blessings they are in possession of, and which no other people on earth enjoy. . . . I will venture to say no man now living will ever see an instance of an American removing to settle in Europe and continuing there."[20] In his first inaugural address in March of 1801, Jefferson observed that his fellow citizens were "kindly separated by nature and a wide ocean from the exterminating havoc of one quarter of the globe; too high minded to endure the degradations of the others, possessing a chosen country, with room enough for our descendants to the thousandth and thousandth generation."[21] And in April of 1809, Jefferson told incoming president James Madison that "we should then have only to include the north [Canada] in our confederacy, which would be of course in the first war, and we should have such an empire for liberty as she has never surveyed since the creation: & I am persuaded no constitution was ever before so well calculated as ours for extensive empire & self-government."[22]

RIGHT OF DISCOVERY

The Right of Discovery, which became known as the Doctrine of Discovery in the U.S. Supreme Court case of *Johnson v. M'Intosh* in 1823,[23] also has religious roots. The concept of Discovery, one of the earliest examples of international law, can be traced back as far as the Holy Land Crusades of the eleventh and twelfth centuries. The Right of Discovery was heavily influenced by the Christian—particularly the Catholic—Church, and the resulting policies were applicable to many geographically imbued activities, including exploration, trade, and colonization.

Several fifteenth-century papal bulls—including the 1493 *Inter caetera* and the subsequent and related Treaty of Tordesillas between Spain and Portugal dividing newly discovered lands in the Americas—are examples of this legal principle. England and France each applied the legal standards of the Right of Discovery to their explorations, subsequent claims, and colonization of North America. This practice did not mean that various national interpretations of the standards were consistent. Sweden and Holland also applied the same legal concepts, albeit on a much smaller scale, to their early North American colonies.[24]

There is little question that Thomas Jefferson was aware of the legal concepts behind the Right of Discovery, even if he did not use the precise phrase in his writings.[25] The principles of Discovery have been divided into ten elements, but this classification scheme is a relatively recent development and was not formally known to Jefferson or his contemporaries.[26] Of those ten elements, at least six had distinct geographical components: first discovery, actual occupancy and current possession, preemption/European title, Indian title, contiguity, and *terra nullius*. Jefferson was aware of the basic principles involved in all these elements, even if he did not refer to them in these terms.

First discovery states that the first European country to "discover" lands unknown to other Europeans assumed property rights over those lands. Actual occupancy and current possession meant that to fully establish "first discovery," the European country had to occupy and possess the new lands, which was often accomplished by building a fort or settlement and occupying that space with soldiers or settlers.

Preemption/European title asserts that the "discovering" European power was granted the power of preemption, that is, the sole right to buy the land from the Native people(s). Indian title was disrupted after first discovery, because indigenous people were considered to have lost full property rights and land ownership: if they ever sold their lands, they could only sell to the government of the European power that held preemptive power. Indian title was, therefore, a severely limited ownership right.

Contiguity meant that a European power had a significant Discovery claim to any lands contiguous or surrounding the areas they actually possessed. One major and important element of contiguity held that first discovery of the mouth of a river gave that European power claim to all the lands drained by it.[27]

Terra nullius—also called *vacuum domicilium*—implies that if lands were not possessed or occupied by any person or nation, or if they were occupied by non-European peoples but not being used in accordance with European legal principles, then the land was considered empty and open to First Discovery claims.[28]

Land ownership conflicts were not always cleanly settled according to the guidelines of the Right of Discovery, and competing claims were not uncommon. Jefferson understood and applied contemporaneous legal principles of the Right of Discovery throughout his public and political career. As a practicing attorney, he handled more than nine hundred legal cases between 1767 and 1774, more than four hundred of which involved land-claim disputes. The vast majority of those land disputes no doubt involved elements of Native American title, as would most all land-claim disputes at that time.[29]

Toward the end of his tenure in Virginia's House of Burgesses in 1776, Jefferson participated in drafting the Virginia State Constitution, wherein the state claimed preemption over all lands in Virginia. In 1779, while Jefferson was in the House of Delegates, Virginia passed a law voiding all past and future purchases of Native lands, claiming an "exclusive right of preemption" over any of those sales. During his two years as governor of Virginia, beginning in 1779, he granted roughly three thousand land titles in the state, the vast majority of which would have involved Discovery issues. During various points in his congressional career, Jefferson was drawn into similar discussions. In 1777 and 1778, he and George Mason were occupied with resolutions planning the sale of lands north and west of the Ohio River to future settlers. Jefferson was intimately involved in what became the federal Land Ordinance of 1784, which considered the ceding of land claims on some western portions of Virginia to Congress.

While serving as secretary of state from 1789 to 1793, Jefferson drew on various principles of the Right of Discovery for the purpose of purchasing Native lands. In 1790, assessing a land ownership conflict between the state of Georgia and Native tribal rights, he wrote:

> The state of Georgia having granted to certain companies of
> individuals a tract of country within their chartered limits, whereof
> the Indian right has never yet been acquired, with a proviso in
> the grant which implies that those individuals may take measures

for extinguishing the Indian right under the authority of that government, it becomes a question How far this grant is good.

A society taking possession of a vacant country, and declaring they mean to occupy it, does thereby appropriate to themselves, as prime occupants, what was before common. A practice introduced since the discovery of America authorises them to go farther, and to fix the limits which they assume to themselves; and it seems for the common good to admit this right to a moderate and reasonable extent. If the country, instead of being altogether vacant, is thinly occupied by another nation, the right of the natives forms an exception to that of the new-comers; that is to say, these will only have a right against all other nations except the natives: consequently they have the exclusive privilege of acquiring the native right by purchase or other just means. This is called the right of pre-emption; and is become a principle of the law of nations, fundamental with respect to America.—There are but two means of acquiring the native title. 1. War; for even war may sometimes give a just title. 2. Contract, or treaty.[30]

Jefferson's two terms as president, and his accompanying involvement in Discovery issues, were crowned by the Louisiana Purchase, the Lewis and Clark expedition, and the plans to develop a settlement at the mouth of the Columbia River in the Pacific Northwest.[31]

NATURAL LAW

Natural law is a heterogeneous and sometimes loosely defined set of concepts, including elements of ethics, morality, civil law, and politics.[32] It is a scaffold for social order in situations where the authority of ancestral or tribal ties has been weakened.[33] Theories of natural law are not as clearly underpinned by geographical considerations as other antecedents of Manifest Destiny, yet Thomas Jefferson managed to make a connection. He was certainly schooled, as were many of his political contemporaries, in those elements of natural law pertaining to civil law and politics, particularly the works of Montesquieu and Locke.

In June of 1800, Jefferson wrote, "nor is it in physics alone that we shall be found to differ from the other hemisphere. I strongly suspect that our geographical peculiarities may call for a different code of natural law to govern relations with other nations from that which the conditions of Europe have given rise there."[34]

In June of 1817, he expounded again on these matters, asserting that "if he [God] has made it a law in the nature of man to pursue his own happiness, he has left him free in the choice of place as well as mode; and we may safely call on the whole body of English jurists to produce the map on which Nature has traced, for each individual, the geographical line which she forbids him to cross in pursuit of happiness."[35]

LOUISIANA PURCHASE

The historical details of the Louisiana Purchase and Thomas Jefferson's involvement have been discussed at great length elsewhere. The acquisition of these lands stemmed from the Right of Discovery and the assertion of a future Manifest Destiny.[36] This signal "real-estate deal" was not a direct purchase of land, but rather of regional Discovery Rights from France and Spain, of which Jefferson was acutely aware. As has been previously noted, the price tag was actually far more than the fifteen million dollar figure frequently cited, due to payments to Native American tribes for their lands within the area of the Purchase.[37]

It is not known which specific maps were used in the planning stages leading to the Purchase, but the 1802 version of Aaron Arrowsmith's *A Map Exhibiting all the New Discoveries in the Interior Parts of North America* has been suggested as one of the likely candidates (fig. 17).[38] Given Jefferson's fondness for Arrowsmith's work, and based on several other maps Jefferson owned, he was certainly familiar with this imprint.[39]

Jefferson's thoughts were clearly focused on such issues prior to the Louisiana Purchase Treaty of April 1803, and thereafter he was characteristically engrossed gathering information about the newly acquired territory, and quickly discovered that the books in his own "legendary" library were not adequate for the task. Perhaps reminiscent of Marbois's queries, which prompted the ultimate publication of *Notes on the State of Virginia,* Jefferson prepared an initial list of seventeen queries to be sent to select individuals with knowledge of the new region. He asked Albert Gallatin, then secretary of the treasury and a man quite familiar with the importance of maps, to look at those queries, and subsequently expanded the initial list to forty-five. That list was then sent to four individuals Jefferson selected to provide advice: William C. C. Claiborne (English-born surveyor and eventually first governor of Louisiana), Daniel Clark Jr. (a merchant and United States consular agent in New Orleans), William Dunbar (Scottish-born explorer, naturalist, and astronomer), and Ephraim Kirby (first Superior Court judge of the Mississippi Territory). Each of these recipients, in turn, talked with their own "consultants" in preparing their responses, with the most detailed of these received from Claiborne, who managed to get through thirty-six of the forty-five queries.[40]

Many of Jefferson's original queries—at least eleven of seventeen by my count—were geographically and cartographically based. Query 17 from that list dealt specifically with mapping: "What are the best maps, general or particular, of the whole or parts of the province? Copies of them if to be had in print."[41]

It is clear that Jefferson was assessing the geographic and cartographic details of the Purchase, and accelerated his efforts after the treaty was signed. In November of 1803, in his *Account of Louisiana,* he noted:

> Of the province of Louisiana no general map, sufficiently correct to be depended upon, has been published, nor has any yet been procured, from a private source. It is indeed probable, that surveys have never been made upon so extensive a scale as to afford the means of laying down the various regions of a country, which, in some of its parts, appears to have been but imperfectly explored.

He then went on to assert:

> The precise boundaries of Louisiana, westwardly of the Mississippi, though very extensive, are at present involved in some obscurity. Data are equally wanting to assign with precision its northern extent. From the source of the Mississippi, it is bounded eastwardly by the middle of the channel of that river to the 31st degree of latitude: thence, it is asserted upon very strong grounds, that according to its limits, when formerly possessed by France, it stretches to the east, as far, at least, as the river Perdigo, which runs into the bay of Mexico, eastward of the river Mobile.[42]

As these brief excerpts suggest, most of this document relates to the geography of the region.

As to any specific maps Jefferson used to assess current information about the area of the Louisiana Purchase, his "Limits and Bounds of Louisiana" dated 15 January 1804, on deposit in the archives of the American Philosophical Society, gives a slight clue. Jefferson observed:

> I possess three ancient maps which mark the Rio bravo & it's Eastern branch as the dividing boundary between Louisiana & Mexico. 1. [Herman] Moll's map of the West Indies & adjacent countries. 2. Moll's map of Louisiana, etc. published in 1720, in which the South Western parts of Louisiana are said to be copied from a French map published in Paris in 1718, and 3. [Johann Baptist] Homann's Spanish map of Louisiana of about the same date.[43]

LEWIS AND CLARK EXPEDITION

As Jefferson was ruminating on the actual boundaries of the Louisiana Purchase, he was also considering how to explore this new territory (and regions beyond), how to establish legal claims—that is, Discovery Rights—to the Pacific Northwest, and how the fabled Northwest Passage might be found.[44] The idea of a watercourse running the width of the North American continent had been part of geographical lore for more than two centuries.[45] Although Jefferson was certainly interested in expanding commerce, he was similarly concerned with increasing the territories of the United States.

Jefferson's 20 June 1803 letter to Meriwether Lewis, quoted at length in chapter 4, offered specific details and instructions, with these telling charges among them:

> Your observations are to be taken with great pains and accuracy; to be entered distinctly & intelligibly for others as well as yourself; to comprehend all the elements necessary, with the aid of the usual tales, to fix the latitude and longitude of the places at which they were taken; and are to be rendered to the war-office, for the purpose of having the calculations made concurrently by proper persons within the U.S. . . .

> And, considering the interest which every nation has in extending & strengthening the authority of reason & justice among the people around them, it will be useful to acquire what knolege you

can of the state of morality, religion, & information among them; as it may better enable those who may endeavor to civilize & instruct them, to adapt their measures to the existing notions & practices of those on whom they are to operate. . . .

Should you reach the Pacific ocean, inform yourself of the circumstances which may decide whether the furs of those parts may not be collected as advantageously at the head of the Missouri (convenient as is supposed to the waters of the Colorado and Oregan or Columbia) as at Nootka Sound, or any other point of that coast; and that trade be consequently conducted through the Missouri and United States more beneficially than by the circumnavigation now practiced.[46]

Although it is true that exploration was already expanding westward along the Missouri River before Lewis and Clark returned with their notes and maps, this does not invalidate the assertion that the Right of Discovery was at play in the nation's continental expansion. As detailed histories and Lewis and Clark's journals attest,[47] their journey bolstered U.S. claims of ownership of the Pacific Northwest.[48]

MAPPING MANIFEST DESTINY

Spanish, French, Russian, and British maps of the sixteenth, seventeenth, and eighteenth centuries all contained early images of North America—and hence the eventual territory of the United States.[49] John Melish's *Map of the United States with the contiguous British & Spanish Possessions Compiled from the latest & best Authorities,* which appeared in 1816, is considered one of the earliest clearly foreshadowing Manifest Destiny (fig. 25),[50] and is the first wall map to show the new nation from coast to coast.[51] In Melish's own words:

When this extract was written, it was intended to carry the map no farther west than the ridge dividing the waters falling into the Gulf of Mexico, from those falling into the Pacific Ocean. A subsequent view of the subject pointed out the propriety of adding the two western sheets, so as to carry it to the Pacific Ocean. For this part excellent materials were procured. Part of this territory unquestionably belongs to the United States. To present a picture of it was desirable in every point of view. The map so constructed,

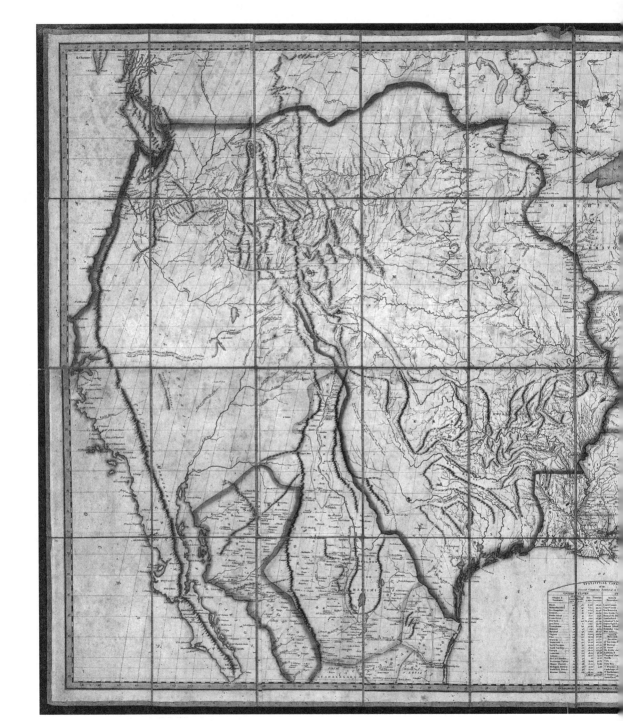

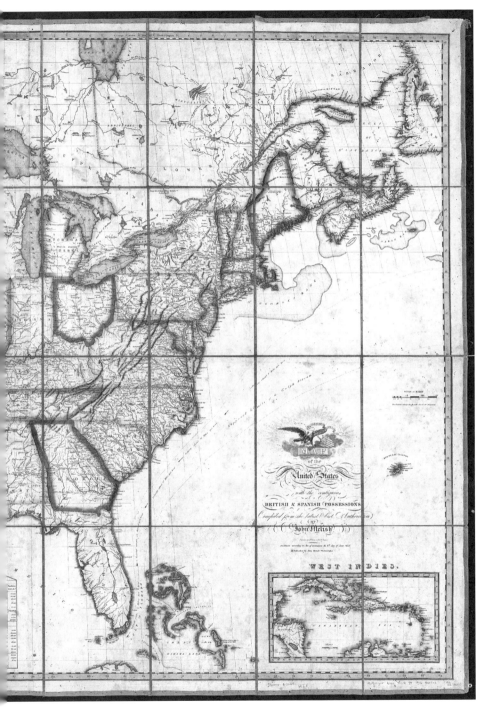

FIGURE 25.
Map of the United States with the contiguous British & Spanish Possessions Compiled from the latest & best Authorities, by John Melish, published in Philadelphia, 1816. This was the first large-scale map produced in the United States showing the entire country from coast to coast. (Albert and Shirley Small Special Collections Library, University of Virginia)

shows at a glance the whole extent of the United States territory from sea to sea; and, in tracing the probable expansion of the human race from east to west, the mind finds an agreeable resting place on its western limits. The view is complete, and leaves nothing to be wished for. . . .

. . . The vast extent of the United States territory—the fertility of the soil—the salubrity of the climate—the magnitude of the rivers and lakes . . . and the view of the whole as being the habitation of men among whom self-government has for the first time had a fair chance of successful experiment.[52]

As we have seen, Jefferson knew Melish, a Scottish mapmaker and publisher then residing and working in Philadelphia who sent the former president a copy of both the aforementioned map and his 1816 publication, *Geographical Description of the United States with the continuous British and Spanish Possessions, intended as an Accompaniment to Melish's Map of these Countries.* The two men had been correspondents for some years prior to the 1816 map. As noted in chapter 5, Jefferson congratulated Melish on the quality of his work and offered critical remarks on this seminal map.[53]

Jefferson's connections to the concept of Manifest Destiny, along with his interest in cartography and the use of maps, point to earlier, portending images, including the detailed planning for the Lewis and Clark expedition (discussed in chapter 4). A number of maps were crucial to that process, including works by Jean Baptiste Bourguignon d'Anville, Aaron Arrowsmith, James Cook, Andrew Ellicott, Nicholas King, Guillaume Delisle, Alexander Mackenzie, John Mitchell, David Thompson, and George Vancouver.[54]

Guillaume Delisle's early-eighteenth-century maps of North America were among the most influential of the time, and also served as sources for John Mitchell's 1755 map. Delisle, a key figure in the development of French cartography, was a master mapmaker, whereas Mitchell, a physician and botanist, is known only for a single—albeit historically highly significant—map.[55] Arrowsmith was a prolific and well-respected English mapmaker and engraver, and his works were favorites of Jefferson, found among the group of continental maps hanging in the great entrance hall at Monticello.[56] Nicholas King, an English immigrant from a family of surveyors, was a mapmaker whose

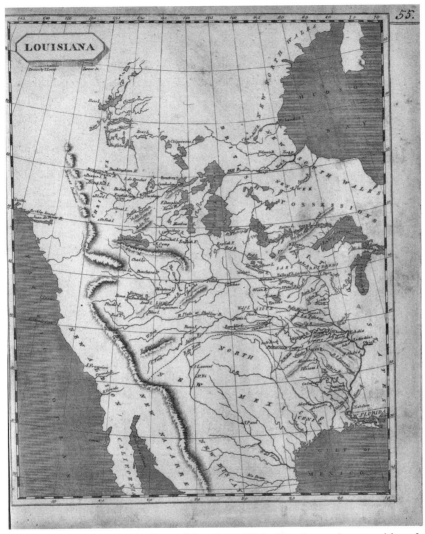

FIGURE 26. *Louisiana,* by Samuel Lewis, published by Aaron Arrowsmith and Samuel Lewis in *A New and Elegant General Atlas,* 1804. (David Rumsey Map Collection)

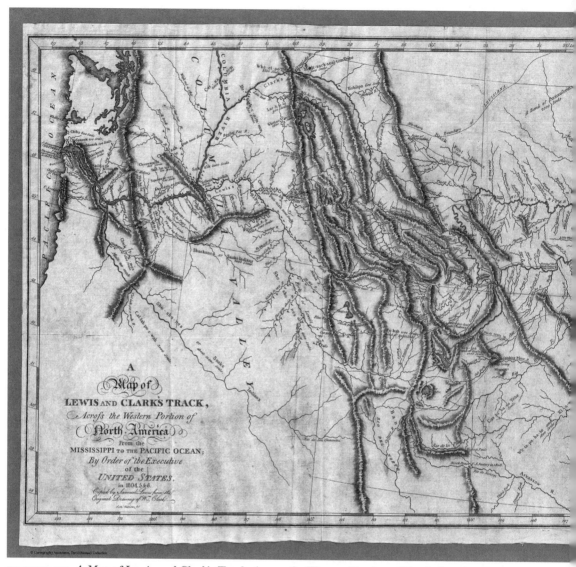

FIGURE 27. *A Map of Lewis and Clark's Track, Across the Western Portion of North America From the Mississippi to the Pacific Ocean; By Order of the Executive of the United States, in 1804, 5 & 6. Copied by Samuel Lewis from the Original Drawing of Wm. Clark,* which appears in *History Of The Expedition Under The Command Of Captains Lewis And Clark, To The Sources Of The Missouri, Thence Across The Rocky Mountains And Down The River Columbia To The Pacific Ocean. Performed During The Years 1804–5–6,* by Paul Allen, Nicolas Biddle, William Clark, and Meriwether Lewis, published in Philadelphia, 1814. (David Rumsey Map Collection)

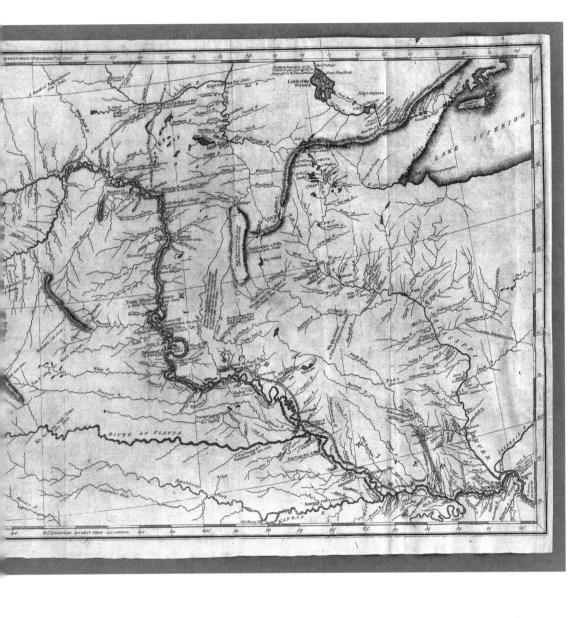

skills Jefferson employed on numerous occasions. King has been described as a "copyist," but this understates his abilities, and he often enhanced and compiled those works he used. Jefferson named King the first official surveyor of the city of Washington, D.C., in 1803.[57] Samuel Lewis, a native Pennsylvanian, was a geographer, publisher, and draftsman. He had corresponded with Jefferson on a number of occasions and was also a contributor to Aaron Arrowsmith's atlases. Andrew Ellicott, another Pennsylvanian, also worked for Jefferson on numerous occasions and taught Meriwether Lewis surveying in preparation for his explorations with William Clark.[58]

Jefferson's insistence on detailed cartographic preparation as part of the expeditionary planning process was crucial to the success of the mission.[59] This is evident in a portion of Albert Gallatin's letter to Jefferson in March of 1803, quoted at length in chapter 4.[60] As noted there, it is not clear precisely which three of Arrowsmith's maps referenced by Gallatin were actually used, but it is likely that two of them were the 1795 and 1802 issues of *A Map Exhibiting all the New Discoveries in the Interior Parts of North America*. Another likely candidate—mentioned above in the context of the Louisiana Purchase—is one of the large wall maps that hangs in Monticello's entry hall, the 1802 issue of Arrowsmith's *A Map of the United States of North America Drawn From a number of Critical Researches*.[61]

Of those maps used in planning the expedition, a number visually foreshadow the notion of Manifest Destiny: Guillaume Delisle's 1718 *Carte de la Louisiane et du Cours du Mississipi* (fig. 20); John Mitchell's 1755 *Map of the British and French Dominions in North America* (fig. 21); Aaron Arrowsmith's aforementioned 1802 *Map Exhibiting all the New Discoveries in the Interior Parts of North America* (fig. 17); and Nicholas King's 1803 untitled manuscript map of western North America (fig. 16). Two other maps that should similarly be considered are Samuel Lewis's 1804 map *Louisiana* (fig. 26), published as part of an Arrowsmith atlas, and a second map compiled by Lewis, a product of the expedition itself, copied from William Clark's original drawing—the 1814 *Map of Lewis and Clark's Track, Across the Western Portion of North America From the Mississippi to the Pacific Ocean* (fig. 27). These were selected, among others, for their individual historical importance, the particular areas of North America covered, and their ties to Jefferson's planning and the execution of the Lewis and Clark expedition.

Jefferson was an integral part of the history of the nation's territorial expansions during the late eighteenth and early nineteenth centuries. He was inextricably tied to the roots of Manifest Destiny. His knowledge of geography and cartography was crucial to his role, and an essential component of those ties. He understood not only that existing maps were crucial for the successful planning of an exploration, but that map production was an important product of the endeavors, and facilitated future scientific development, land claims, and commerce.

7

GEOGRAPHICAL
MISCELLANIES

❊ ❊ ❊
❊ ❊
❊

geography, n.
a. The science which has for its object the description of the earth's
surface, treating of its form and physical features, its natural and political
divisions, the climate, productions, population, etc., of the various
countries. It is frequently divided into mathematical geography, physical
geography, and political geography.
b. The study of a subject in its geographical aspects.
— Oxford English Dictionary

Jefferson's view of geography was expansive and intersected
with his diverse scientific interests, including agronomy, an-
thropology, archaeology, astronomy, botany, chorography,
ethnology, geology, horology, linguistics, meteorology, paleontology, topography, and zoology.[1]
Those interests frequently overlapped within his writings—as can
be seen in the excerpts in this chapter—and coincided with the early
notion of geography as the "mother of all sciences." That generalization
ceased to be convincing as academic specializations increased during
the latter part of the nineteenth century.[2] Unquestionably, geography—
and, in particular, physical geography—was part of a classic education
and an important subject for Jefferson in both secondary school and
university.[3]
  Jefferson's interests in agriculture, rooted in his lifelong involvement
with farming and the management of Monticello, are well known. An
edited version of his *Farm Book* contains not only a facsimile of the actual document but a detailed "Commentary and relevant Extracts from
Other Writings," with entries outlining information pertaining to the
existing farm buildings, animals, ground preparation, crops (including
tobacco), lands, and regional details of the Rivanna River (including

mills, dam, and canal).[4] A similar edited version of Jefferson's *Garden Book* is equally expansive with regard to geographical details.[5]

Jefferson's archaeological interests have likewise been well established.[6] He has been called the "father of American archaeology," and he is credited with initiating the principle of stratigraphy—the study of rock layers and layering—in archaeological excavation.[7] These principles are highlighted in Jefferson's Query XI of *Notes on the State of Virginia,* "A description of the Indians":

> Every one will readily seize the circumstances above related, which militate against the opinion, that it covered the bones only of persons fallen in battle; and against the tradition also, which would make it the common sepulchre of a town, in which the bodies were placed upright, and touching each other. Appearances certainly indicate that it has derived both origin and growth from the accustomary collection of bones, and deposition of them together; that the first collection had been deposited on the common surface of the earth, a few stones put over it, and then a covering of earth, that the second had been laid on this, had covered more or less of it in proportion to the number of bones, and was then also covered with earth; and so on. The following are the particular circumstances which give it this aspect. 1. The number of bones. 2. Their confused position. 3. Their being in different strata. 4. The strata in one part having no correspondence with those in another. 5. The different states of decay in these strata, which seem to indicate a difference in the time of inhumation. 6. The existence of infant bones among them.[8]

Jefferson's interest in astronomy—clearly tied to his concerns with land surveying and the demarcation of boundaries—began when he was a young man and continued through much of his adult life.[9] His personal classification of his Great Library included a section on astronomy, listed under philosophy and just preceding the section on geography.[10] His letters are diffusely laced with references to the importance of education in astronomy and astronomical observations. This connection seems reasonable, since astronomy and geography were commonly taught together and were certainly intellectually interdependent.[11]

While governor of Virginia, Jefferson demonstrated his understanding of the importance of astronomical observation for land surveying in a letter he wrote to Joseph Reed, then president of Pennsylvania's Supreme Executive Council (the equivalent of a state governor):

> I have been honoured with your Excellency's letter proposing the actual extension of our mutual boundary. I presume . . . that the Boundaries are to be run on the principles therein proposed. No mode of determining the extent of the five degrees of longitude from Delaware river in the latitude of Mason and Dixons line having been pointed out by your Excellency I shall venture to propose that this be determined by Astronomical Observations to be made at or near the two extremities of the Line as being in our opinion the most certain and unexceptionable mode of determining that point which being fixed every thing else will be easy. . . .
> We will send to the Westward the most necessary Instruments which we suppose to be a good time piece, Telescopes and a transit Instrument and hope it will be convenient for you to furnish what may be necessary at the Eastern End.[12]

In a 1785 letter to Ezra Stiles, then president of Yale University, Jefferson emphasized the general importance of astronomical learning:

> I have long deferred doing myself the honour of writing to you, wishing for an opportunity to accompany my letter with a copy of the Bibliotheque Physico-œconomique, a book published here lately in four small volumes, and which gives an account of all the improvements in the arts which have been made for some years past. . . . I accompany it with the volumes of the Connoissance des tems for the years 1781. 1784. 1785. 1786. 1787. But why, you will ask, do I send you old almanachs, which are proverbially useless? Because in these publications have appeared from time to time some of the most precious things in astronomy. I have searched out those particular volumes which might be valuable to you on this account. That of 1781. contains de la Caille's catalogue of fixed stars reduced to the commencement of that year, [299] and a table of the Aberrations and Nutations of the principal stars. 1784. contains the same catalogue with the Nebuleuses of Messier. 1785 contains the famous catalogue of Flamsteed with the positions of the stars reduced to the beginning of the year 1784. and which supersedes the use of that immense book. 1786 gives you Euler's Lunar tables

corrected; and 1787 the tables for the planet Herschel. The two last needed not an apology, as not being within the description of old almanachs. It is fixed on grounds which scarcely admit a doubt that the planet Herschel was seen by Mayer in the year 1756. and was considered by him as one of the Zodiacal stars, and as such arranged in his catalogue, being the 964th. which he describes. This 964th. of Mayer has been since missing, and the calculations for the planet Herschel shew that it should have been at the time of Mayer's observation where he places his 964th. star. The volume of 1787. gives you Mayer's Catalogue of the Zodiacal stars.[13]

In December of 1811, as part of his ongoing communications with Bishop Madison, Jefferson wrote:

> I thank you for mr Lambard's [Lambert's] calculation on my observations of the late eclipse of the sun. I have been for some time rubbing up my Mathematics from the rust contracted by 50. years pursuits of a different kind . . . I have a fine theodolite & Equatorial both by Ramsden, a Hadley's circle of Borda, a fine meridian and horizon as you know. once ascertaining the dip of my horizon I can use the circle, as at sea, without an artificial horizon.[14]

Bishop Madison's *Map of Virginia Formed from Actual Surveys* was the first map compiled, engraved, and published in the state (fig. 28). Madison did not produce the map himself, although he guided the production. The map was well known to Jefferson, who had been asked to examine the map prior to its release.[15] A second edition did not appear until 1818, after Bishop Madison's death.

Jefferson fully understood the importance of measurements of longitude for his astronomical observations. In June of 1812, he wrote to Andrew Ellicott:

> I have duly received your favor of the 3d and thank you in advance for that of a copy of your observations, when they will be published. There always existed a doubt whether the source of the Savannah was not north of the 35th degree, which your labors have now removed. A great deal is yet wanting to ascertain the true geography of our country; more indeed as to its longitudes than latitudes. Towards this we have done too little for ourselves and depended too long on the ancient and inaccurate observations of

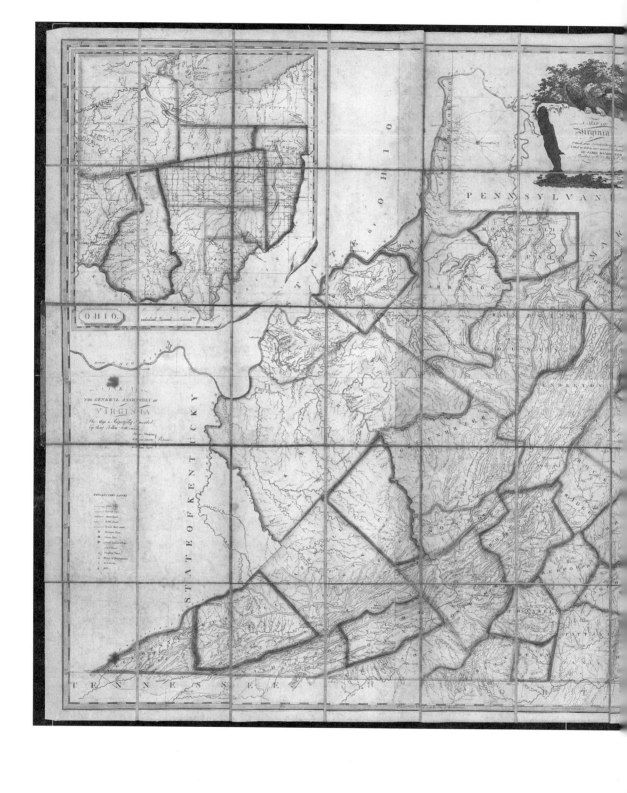

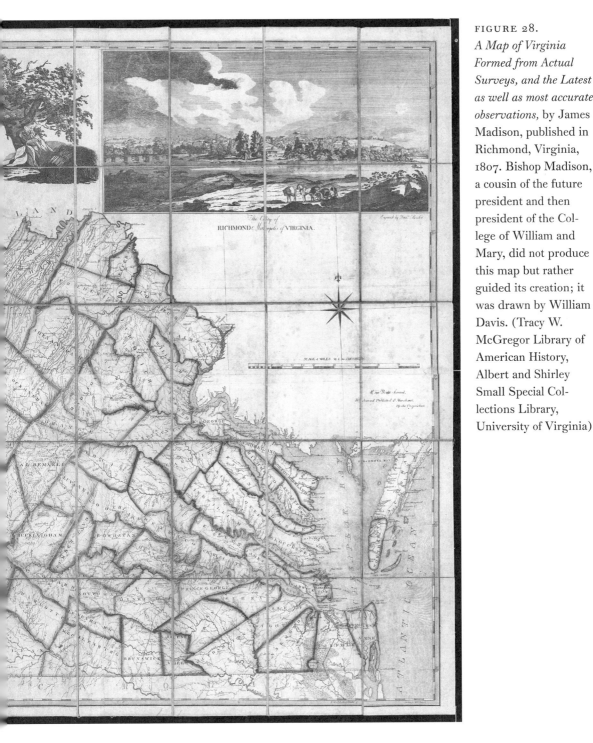

FIGURE 28.
*A Map of Virginia
Formed from Actual
Surveys, and the Latest
as well as most accurate
observations,* by James
Madison, published in
Richmond, Virginia,
1807. Bishop Madison,
a cousin of the future
president and then
president of the Col-
lege of William and
Mary, did not produce
this map but rather
guided its creation; it
was drawn by William
Davis. (Tracy W.
McGregor Library of
American History,
Albert and Shirley
Small Special Col-
lections Library,
University of Virginia)

other nations. You are wiping off this reproach, and will, I hope, be long continued in that work. All this will be for a future race when the superlunary geography will have become the object of my contemplations. Yet I do not wish it the less. On the same principle on which I am still planting trees, to yield their shade and ornament half a century hence.[16]

Jefferson's *Notes on the State of Virginia* is not merely a pioneering work of history and geography, but also a regional, descriptive chorography. Two of his best known geological and topographical observations from that volume discuss the passage of the Potomac River through the Blue Ridge Mountains at Harper's Ferry, and Natural Bridge, located in Rockbridge County, Virginia. In Query IV, Jefferson observed in near-poetic detail:

> The passage of the Patowmac through the Blue ridge is perhaps one of the most stupendous scenes in nature. You stand on a very high point of land. On your right comes up the Shenandoah, having ranged along the foot of the mountain an hundred miles to seek a vent. On your left approaches the Patowmac, in quest of a passage also. In the moment of their junction they rush together against the mountain, rend it asunder, and pass off to the sea. The first glance of this scene hurries our senses into the opinion, that this earth has been created in time, that the mountains were formed first, that the rivers began to flow afterwards, that in this place particularly they have been dammed up by the Blue ridge of mountains, and have formed an ocean which filled the whole valley; that continuing to rise they have at length broken over at this spot, and have torn the mountain down from its summit to its base. The piles of rock on each hand, but particularly on the Shenandoah, the evident marks of their disrupture and avulsion from their beds by the most powerful agents of nature, corroborate the impression. But the distant finishing which nature has given to the picture is of a very different character. It is a true contrast to the fore-ground. It is as placid and delightful, as that is wild and tremendous. For the mountain being cloven asunder, she presents to your eye, through the cleft, a small catch of smooth blue horizon, at an infinite distance in the plain country, inviting you, as it were, from

the riot and tumult roaring around, to pass through the breach and participate of the calm below. Here the eye ultimately composes itself; and that way too the road happens actually to lead. You cross the Patowmac above the junction, pass along its side through the base of the mountain for three miles, its terrible precipices hanging in fragments over you, and within about 20 miles reach Frederic town and the fine country round that. This scene is worth a voyage across the Atlantic. Yet here, as in the neighbourhood of the natural bridge, are people who have passed their lives within half a dozen miles, and have never been to survey these monuments of a war between rivers and mountains, which must have shaken the earth itself to its center.[17]

He continued in Query V:

The Natural bridge, the most sublime of Nature's works, though not comprehended under the present head, must not be pretermitted. It is on the ascent of a hill, which seems to have been cloven through its length by some great convulsion. The fissure, just at the bridge, is, by some admeasurements, 270 feet deep, by others only 205. It is about 45 feet wide at the bottom, and 90 feet at the top; this of course determines the length of the bridge, and its height from the water. Its breadth in the middle, is about 60 feet, but more at the ends, and the thickness of the mass at the summit of the arch, about 40 feet. A part of this thickness is constituted by a coat of earth, which gives growth to many large trees. The residue, with the hill on both sides, is one solid rock of lime-stone. The arch approaches the Semi-elliptical form; but the larger axis of the ellipsis, which would be the cord of the arch, is many times longer than the transverse. Though the sides of this bridge are provided in some parts with a parapet of fixed rocks, yet few men have resolution to walk to them and look over into the abyss. . . . If the view from the top be painful and intolerable, that from below is delightful in an equal extreme. . . . so beautiful an arch, so elevated, so light, and springing as it were up to heaven, the rapture of the spectator is really indescribable! The fissure continuing narrow, deep, and streight for a considerable distance above and below the bridge, opens a short but very pleasing view of the North mountain on one side, and Blue ridge on the other, at the distance each of them of about five miles. This bridge is in the county of Rock bridge, to which it has given name, and affords a public and commodious passage over a valley, which cannot be crossed elsewhere for a considerable distance. The stream passing under it is called Cedar creek. It is a water of James river, and sufficient in the driest seasons to turn a grist-mill, though its fountain is not more than two miles above.[18]

Jefferson's enduring interest in linguistics is easily coupled with his interest in geography.[19] He was conscious of the influence of geographical features when assessing language disparities among Native Americans:

> The Monacans and their friends, better known latterly by the name of Tuscaroras, were probably connected with the Massawomecs, or Five Nations. For though we are told their languages were so different that the intervention of interpreters was necessary between them, yet do we also learn that the Erigas, a nation formerly inhabiting on the Ohio, were of the same original stock with the Five Nations, and that they partook also of the Tuscarora language. Their dialects might, by long separation, have become so unlike as to be unintelligible to one another. We know that in 1712, the Five Nations received the Tuscaroras into their confederacy, and made them the Sixth Nation. They received the Meherrins and Tuteloes also into their protection: and it is most probable, that the remains of many other of the tribes, of whom we find no particular account, retired westwardly in like manner, and were incorporated with one or other of the western tribes.[20]

Jefferson's meteorological observations spanned more than five decades.[21] The National Weather Service has called him the "father of weather observers," and he maintained a serious interest in the subject for many years.[22] In January of 1817, he wrote:

> Having been stationary at home since 1809, with opportunity and leisure to keep a meteorological diary, with a good degree of exactness, this has been done . . . from January 1, 1810 to December 31, 1816, I proceed to analyze it in the varius ways, and to deduce the general results, which are of principal effect in the estimate of

climate. The observations, three thousand nine hundred and five, in the whole, were taken before sunrise every day; and again between three and four o'clock P.M. . . .

The table of thermometrical observations, shews the particular temperature of the different years from 1810 to 1816 inclusive. . . .

It is a common opinion that the climates of the several States, of our Union, have undergone a sensible change since the dates of their first settlements; that the degrees both of cold and heat are moderated. The same opinion prevails as to Europe; and the facts gleaned from history give reason to believe that, since the time of Augustus Caesar, the climate of Italy, for example has changed regularly, at a rate of 1° give reason to believe that, since the time of Augustus Caesar, the climate of Italy, for example has changed regularly, at a rate of 1° of Fahrenheit's thermometer for every century. . . .

In this separate table I state the relation which each particular wind appears to have with rain or snow . . . The table consequently shows the degree in which any particular wind enters as an element into the generation of rain, in combination with the temperature of the air, state of clouds, &c.

An estimate of climate may be otherwise made from the advance of the spring, as manifested by animal and vegetable subjects. Their first appearance has been observed as follows. . . .

Another index of climate may be sought in the temperature of the waters issuing from fountains . . .

Lastly, to close the items which designate climate, the latitude of Monticello is to be added, which by numerous observations lately made with a Borda's circle of 5 inches radius, with nonius divisions.[23]

Five years later, Jefferson remained fixed on the state of meteorological science, writing in September of 1822:

Of all the departments of science no one seems to have been less advanced for the last hundred years than that of meteorology. The new chemistry indeed has given us a new principle of the generation of rain, by proving water to be a composition of different gases, and has aided our theory of meteoric lights. Electricity stands where Dr. Franklin's early discoveries placed it, except with its new modification of galvanism. But the phenomena of snow, hail, halo, aurora borealis, haze, looming, etc., are as yet very imperfectly understood. I am myself an empiric in natural philosophy, suffering my faith to go no further than my facts. I am pleased, however, to see the efforts of hypothetical speculation, because by the collisions of different hypotheses, truth may be elicited and science advanced in the end. This sceptical disposition does not permit me to say whether your hypothesis for looming and the floating volumes of warm air occasionally perceived, may or may not be confirmed by future observations. More facts are yet wanting to furnish a solution on which we may rest with confidence. I even doubt as yet whether the looming at sea and at land are governed by the same laws. In this state of uncertainty, I cannot presume either to advise or discourage the publication of your essay.[24]

Jefferson's interests in North American natural history, including elements of paleontology and zoology, can readily be seen in his well-publicized disputes with the French naturalist Georges-Louis Leclerc, Comte de Buffon.[25] In a 1789 letter to Joseph Willard, then president of Harvard University, Jefferson noted:

The return of la Peyrouse (whenever that shall happen) will probably add to our knowlege in Geography, botany and natural history. What a feild have we at our doors to signalize ourselves in! The botany of America is far from being exhausted: it's Mineralogy is untouched, and it's Natural history or Zoology totally mistaken and misrepresented. As far as I have seen there is not one single species of terrestrial birds common to Europe and America, and I question if there be a single species of quadrupeds. (Domestic animals are to be excepted.) It is for such institutions as that over which you preside so worthily, Sir, to do justice to our country, it's productions, and it's genius.[26]

In 1809, commenting on a volume on geography written by Horatio G. Spafford, Jefferson stated:

In passing my eye rapidly over parts of the book, I was struck with two passages, on which I will make observations, not doubting your wish; in any future edition, to render the work as correct as you can. in page 186. you say the potatoe is a native of the US. I presume you speak of the Irish potatoe. I have enquired much into this question, & think I can assure you that plant is not a native of N. America. Zimmerman, in his Geographical Zoology, says it is a native of Guiana; & Clavigero, that the Mexicans got it from S. America, it's native country. the most probable account I have been able to collect is that a vessel of Sr Walter Raleigh's, returning from Guiana, put into the West of Ireland in distress, having on board some potatoes which they called earth apples. that the season of the year, & circumstance of their being already sprouted induced them to give them all out there, and they were no more heard or thought of, till they had been spread considerably into that island, whence they were carried over into England, & therefore called the Irish potatoe. from England they came to the US. bringing their name with them.

the other passage respects the description of the passage of the Potomac through the Blue ridge in the Notes on Virginia. you quote from Volney's account of the US. what his words do not justify. his words are 'on coming from Frederick town one does not see the rich perspective mentioned in the notes of Mr Jefferson. on observing this to him a few days after he informed me he had his information from a French engineer who, during the war of Independance ascended the height of the hills & I concieve that at that elevation the perspective must be as imposing as a wild country, whose horizon has no obstacles, may present.' that the scene described in the Notes is not visible from any part of the road from Frederick town to Harper's ferry is most certain. that road passes along the valley. nor can it be seen from the tavern after crossing the ferry; & we may fairly infer that mr Volney did not ascend the height back of the tavern from which alone it can be seen, but that he pursued his journey from the tavern along the high road. yet he admits that at the elevation of that height the perspective may be as rich as a wild country can present. but you make him 'surprised to find by a view of the spot, that the description was amazingly exaggerated.' but it is evident that mr Volney did not ascend the hill to get a view of the spot, and that he supposes that that height may present as imposing a view as such a country admits. but mr Volney was mistaken in saying I told him

I had recieved the description from a French engineer. by an error of memory he has misapplied to this scene what I mentioned to him as to the Natural bridge.[27]

As these varied passages suggest, Jefferson's sustained interests in a wide range of subjects were nearly unequalled among his contemporaries. And though we cannot know for certain what legacy he envisioned when writing the *Notes on the State of Virginia*,[28] his words and views, and the landscape they conjure, endure to this day, reinforcing the prevailing eighteenth-century notion of geography as the "mother of all sciences."

J efferson's legal and political careers were permeated with concepts of territory: regional, national, and continental. He was intimately involved in land dispute resolution and territorial acquisition and measurement, and figures prominently in most discussions of the early expansion of the United States. Evidence of his chorographic (descriptions or depictions of particular regions), geographic, and cartographic interests and knowledge can be found throughout his adult life. They were manifest in his extensive writings, in his remarkable libraries, in his early legal career. They suffuse the planning and execution of the building of Washington, D.C.; the acquisition and exploration of the Louisiana Territory and the Pacific Northwest; the planning and building of his remarkable home at Monticello; and the creation of the University of Virginia. The size and scope of his geographical library, remarkable as it was, does not fully reflect the crucial importance of geographically related subjects to his ever-growing intellectual pursuits and professional responsibilities.

Jefferson's interest in and use of maps was firmly joined to his command of contemporary geographical information. He understood the value of maps for the filing and resolution of land claims, for the planning and documentation of detailed territorial exploration, and for the development of regional and national commerce.

Jefferson is an iconic example of a "lifelong learner," however trite the phrase may seem. He was not unique among his contemporaries in his formal education or in his geographic instruction as a young man. Geography could, during the mid-to-late eighteenth and early nineteenth centuries, legitimately be considered as the "mother of all sciences," and an integral part of a classical education for young "gentlemen."[1]

Several converging historical trends helped spur Jefferson's interest in and use of maps: a markedly increasing demand for printed maps by an interested public, the need to illustrate the fields of battle relating to the Seven Years War and the American Revolution, and the explorations so crucial—for political, economic and scientific reasons—to the westward expansion of the early republic.

As the eighteenth century came to a close, neither the fledgling nation nor the European imperial powers had adequate information about lands west of the Mississippi, and the public was eager for maps to define as yet unknown territories. Both desires helped feed Jefferson's need for better geographic and cartographic information.

This assessment of Jefferson's significance does not by any means minimize the importance of the myriad talented individuals—William Small, Albert Gallatin, David Rittenhouse, Bishop James Madison, Benjamin Franklin, Andrew Ellicott, Nicholas King, Alexander von Humboldt, to name but a few—who were so important in augmenting Jefferson's expansive and varied scientific interests. Contemporary military leaders, such as George Washington, had requisite interest in and knowledge of terrain and maps. Other landowners, Washington among them, had interests in and practical needs for the techniques and accuracy of land surveying.[2] Some were involved with what would come to be called urban planning and landscape architecture. Other extraordinary expedition planners included Sir Joseph Banks and Alexander Mackenzie. Although university-level academic geography was not yet well developed, professional and scholarly geographers, including the likes of Christoph Daniel Ebeling and his student Alexander von Humboldt, were part of Jefferson's world, his Republic of Letters.

The importance of geography in modern education is clear, and the level of geographical education and training seems to be improving.[3] This is news that Jefferson would applaud. He would have been fascinated by the integration of digital technologies into the study and use of geography and mapping. His reliance on the best geographic and cartographic information available at the time was critical for the early development of the United States, at a time when land and landscape set the stage for our national growth and mythology.

NOTES

❁ ❁ ❁
❁ ❁
❁

Abbreviations

FE   *The Works of Thomas Jefferson,* edited by Paul Leicester Ford (Ford Edition)

ME   *The Writings of Thomas Jefferson,* edited by Andrew A. Lipscomb and Albert Ellery Bergh
for the Thomas Jefferson Memorial Association (Memorial Edition)

PTJ   *Papers of Thomas Jefferson,* Main Series

PTJ-D   *Papers of Thomas Jefferson,* Digital Edition

PTJ-R   *Papers of Thomas Jefferson,* Retirement Series

TJ   Thomas Jefferson

Introduction

1. Stein, *Worlds of Thomas Jefferson,* 61–71. See http://www.monticello.org/site/house-and -gardens/entrance-hall for a discussion of the entrance hall display. The continental wall maps were by Aaron Arrowsmith, a British cartographer, engraver, and publisher whose works Jefferson favored.

2. Bailyn, "Jefferson and the Ambiguities of Freedom," 41; Lewis and Onuf, "American Synecdoche," 125–36.

3. Koelsch, "Thomas Jefferson, American Geographers, and the Uses of Geography," notes, "If indeed Jefferson was 'one of the greatest' of American geographers, one would not know it from examining recent American geographical literature" (276). Donald Jackson's chapter, "A Geographer's Bookshelf," in his *Thomas Jefferson and the Stony Mountains* (86–97), focuses on Jefferson's geographically detailed library holdings. John Logan Allen ties Jefferson's geo-graphical education to his ultimate views of the American West in "Imagining the West."

4. Ristow, *American Maps and Mapmakers.* The "T. H. Jefferson" briefly noted in the text and index is not known to be related to the president.

5. Although the concept of mapmaking clearly precedes the printed map by many millennia, the word "cartography," likely derived from the French *cartographie,* did not become part of the English lexicon until the mid-nineteenth century. It should also be noted that in Jefferson's time maps were rapidly growing in popularity as way-finding devices, where previously the written itinerary had been the dominant means through most of the seventeenth century. See Catherine Delano-Smith, "Milieus of Mobility," in Akerman, *Cartographies of Travel and Navigation,* 16–68.

6. Withers, "Eighteenth-Century Geography"; Mayhew, "Geography in Eighteenth Century British Education."

7. Schulten, *Geographical Imagination,* 126.

8. TJ to Sir Herbert Croft, 30 October 1798, *PTJ-D* (http://rotunda.upress.virginia.edu/found ers/TSJN-01-30-02-0385); original source *PTJ* 30 (1 January 1798–31 January 1799).

9. This definition was copied from an 1830 edition of Johnson's dictionary, published in London by Joseph Ogle Robinson and "stereotyped verbatim from the last folio edition corrected by the doctor." That was the fourth edition, published in 1775, and referenced in Sowerby's catalog of Jefferson's Great Library, which became the core of the Library of Congress. The first edition of Johnson's work was published in 1755.

10. The literature here is enormous and overwhelming. For our purposes, see J. L. Allen's three-volume series *North American Exploration,* Casey's *Representing Place,* and the first two volumes of Meinig's *The Shaping of America* (*Atlantic America, 1492–1800* and *Continental America, 1800–1867*).

11. Mapp, *Elusive West,* 1–16. This is not to ignore the involvements of Russia in the Pacific Northwest, but the conflicts between the Spanish, French, and British were more intricately connected. Mapp clearly states that, during the fifty years between the 1713 Treaty of Utrecht and the 1763 Peace of Paris, the bulk of the western two-thirds of North America were largely unknown and poorly described by European settlers, scouts, and traders.

12. Ronda, "To Acquire What Knoledge You Can."

13. See chapters 1 ("Antiquity to Capitalism," 1–8) and 8 ("Colonial Settlement from Europe," 265–330) of Kain and Baigent, *Cadastral Map.*

14. Monmonier, *Drawing the Line,* 105–47; De Vorsey, *Indian Boundary.*

15. See the introduction to Akerman, *Cartographies of Travel and Navigation* (1–15), and

chapter 2, "Milieus of Mobility" (16–68), by Catherine Delano-Smith.

16. Stein, *Worlds of Thomas Jefferson,* 389.

17. Mark Dimunation, "'The Whole of Recorded Knowledge': Jefferson as Collector and Reader," paper presented at the conference "John Adams and Thomas Jefferson: Libraries, Leadership, and Legacy," 26 June 2009, University of Virginia. (http://www.adamsjefferson.com/ papers/Dimunation_Recorded_Knowledge .pdf). See also D. L. Wilson, *Jefferson's Books.*

18. Brückner, *Geographic Revolution,* "The Geographic Revolution in the Wilderness" (1–15) and "The Surveyed Self" (16–50).

19. Cosgrove, *Geography and Vision,* 3–5. He writes about the conflicts between textual and visual—particularly pictorial—geography: "That association between geography and maps remains strong in the popular mind, whether as rote learning of geographical facts by colouring or locating places on maps, or more recently as the manipulation of spatially referenced data in Geographical Information Science (GIS), is a sign of the continued significance of graphic images in shaping geographical knowledge. But among professional geographers, especially those concerned with social and cultural questions, there is today a marked unease about the association between geography, the pictorial and vision" (3).

20. Brückner, *Geographic Revolution,* 132–34, 144–45. He notes, "Like the travel narrative, natural histories such as John Filson's *Discovery, Settlement, and Present State of Kentucke* (1784), Jeremy Belknap's *History of New Hampshire* (1784), and Thomas Jefferson's *Notes . . .* (1785), also operated inside a narrative framework that begins with a map image (or its verbal approximation) and ends with the assertion of character types" (144). These textual narratives helped to establish local identities.

21. TJ, *Notes* (1972 ed.), xi–xxv. Marbois's

original twenty-two queries, generated some time before 30 November 1780, are cited via *PTJ-D,* Marbois's queries concerning Virginia, before 30 November 1780, (http://rotunda.upress.virginia.edu/founders/TSJN-01-04-02-0197); original source *PTJ* 4 (1 October 1780–24 February 1781). Apparently there were two versions of those queries, including a shorter one numbering sixteen (see Nancy Heywood, "A Draft Copy of 'Notes on the State of Connecticut,'" Massachusetts Historical Society Online: Object of the Month, April 2010; http://www.masshist.org/objects/2010april.php). It is not clear which version of Marbois's queries is earliest, though speculation holds that the longer was the original.

22. See note 17 above. For a summary of Jefferson's various library compilations, see "Thomas Jefferson's Libraries."

23. Gilreath and Wilson, *Thomas Jefferson's Library.*

24. See note 17 above, and Dimunation, "Whole of Recorded Knowledge," 10. A fire on Christmas Eve 1851 destroyed two-thirds of Jefferson's Great Library, the core of the Library of Congress collection. At its bicentennial in 2000, the Library of Congress launched a project to reconstruct the 1815 library.

25. For the beginnings of the American Rectangular Survey, see Hubbard, *American Boundaries,* 181–214. For a short discussion of the founding of the United States Coastal Survey, see Friis, "A Brief Review," 4; Theberge, *The Coast Survey 1807–1867,"* provides a more detailed history.

1. A Surveyor's House

1. Drake, *Nation's Nature;* Mapp, *Elusive West.*

2. Brückner, *Geographic Revolution,* 26.

3. Ibid., 20–25.

4. J. L. Allen, "Imagining the West," 3–8, holds that numerous childhood associations played a substantive role in Jefferson's future skills and course. See also Nichols and Griswold, *Thomas Jefferson, Landscape Architect,* 1–2, who asserted that informal instruction at his father's knee set the groundwork for Jefferson's future geographical endeavors. For a dissenting view, see Jackson, *Thomas Jefferson and the Stony Mountains,* 12. Jackson also notes that it was not clear what books pertaining to geography Jefferson had purchased for his early Shadwell library, which burned.

5. Brückner, *Geographic Revolution,* 16–19, 29. He describes the importance of the written, textual field ledger.

6. Ibid., 26–27.

7. Hughes, *Surveyors and Statesmen,* 84–105, 156–65.

8. Bedini, *Thomas Jefferson: Statesman of Science,* 15; Hayes, *Road to Monticello,* 26–27; a typescript of Peter Jefferson's will and inventory is available at the Albert and Shirley Small Special Collections Library of the University of Virginia (MSS 830).

9. Hickisch, *Peter Jefferson, Gentleman,* 25.

10. Verner, "Fry and Jefferson Map," 69.

11. George Washington's career as a professional surveyor, begun at the age of seventeen for the newly formed Culpeper County, was much more impressive: his name was attached to nearly two hundred surveys (Hughes, *Surveyors and Statesmen,* 93).

12. Ganter, "William Small"; Hayes, *Road to Monticello,* 43–56; Malone, *Jefferson and His Time,* 1:49–61.

13. Bedini, *Thomas Jefferson: Statesman of Science,* 60.

14. Ibid., 61.

15. Ibid., 35–40; Raphael, "Thomas Jefferson, Astronomer".

16. Reinhold, "The Quest for 'Useful Knowledge,'" 128–30.

17. R. J. Miller, *Native America,* 60–61. He writes, "Out of the 941 cases Jefferson handled during his legal career, 429 of them were land-claim disputes" (60).

18. Gaines, "Unpublished Thomas Jefferson Map."

19. TJ to the Rev. James Madison and Robert Andrews, 31 March 1781, *PTJ-D* (http://rotunda.upress.virginia.edu/founders/TSJN-01-05-02-0393); original source *PTJ* 5 (25 February 1781–20 May 1781).

20. Bedini, *Thomas Jefferson: Statesman of Science,* 499–501.

21. Ibid., 228–30. For images of Jefferson's scientific instruments, many of which relate to surveying and other geographical interests, see Stein, *Worlds of Thomas Jefferson,* 350–64.

22. Stein, *Worlds of Thomas Jefferson,* 373–76; TJ to Benjamin Vaughan, 23 July 1788, *PTJ-D* (http://rotunda.upress.virginia.edu/founders/TSJN-01-13-02-0290); original source *PTJ* 13 (March–7 October 1788). In this letter, Jefferson spends more time discussing hygrometers.

23. TJ, "Draft of 'An Ordinance Establishing a Land Office for the United States,'" FE 4:406–7.

24. "Report of a Committee to Establish a Land Office," ME 3:475–83. Jefferson was well aware of the significance of magnetic variation and its importance for an accurate land survey (see Warner, "True North," 378–80).

25. TJ to David Hartley, 5 September 1785, *PTJ-D* (http://rotunda.upress.virginia.edu/founders/TSJN-01-08-02-0373); original source *PTJ* 8 (25 February–31 October 1785). David Hartley was also responsible for drafting what has become known as the "Jefferson-Hartley" map, depicting fourteen newly planned states in the Northwest Territory. Those divisions were not in the plans formally approved by Congress. That map was an amalgamation of efforts, and it is not

possible to know precisely how much Jefferson was involved in its production; see the "Editorial Note, Plan for the Western Territory" in *PTJ-D* (http://rotunda.upress.virginia.edu/founders/TSJN-01-06-02-0420-0001); original source *PTJ* 6 (21 May 1781–1 March 1784).

26. See the notes at the end of Jefferson's 8 November 1791 "Report on Public Lands" in *PTJ-D* (http://rotunda.upress.virginia.edu/founders/TSJN-01-22-02-0258); original source *PTJ* 22 (6 August 1791–31 December 1791).

27. This is not to be confused with the formal founding of the General Land Office, which was created in 1812 within the U.S. Treasury Department.

28. Bedini, *Jefferson Stone;* J. H. Pratt, "American Prime Meridians," 234–37.

29. J. H. Pratt, "American Prime Meridians," 322–24.

30. Stanley, "Ferdinand R. Hassler," 17–20. Others considered for the position include Isaac Briggs and Andrew Ellicott (both of whom helped train Meriwether Lewis for the landmark exploration), John Garrett, James Madison (the future fourth president), Nicholas King and Joshua Moore (the first surveyor of the city of Washington, and a young astronomer who accompanied him when he emigrated from England to the early republic in 1793), and Robert Patterson (an Irish immigrant, astronomer, and a professor of mathematics, chemistry, and natural philosophy at the University of Pennsylvania).

31. Ibid., 17–20; Friis, "A Brief Review," 70–72; see also the previous note. Hassler did not actually begin surveying the New York harbor until 1817. (See Theberge, *The Coast Survey 1807–1867.*)

32. TJ to Benjamin Rush, 23 September 1800, *PTJ-D* (http://rotunda.upress.virginia.edu/founders/TSJN-01-32-02-0102); original source *PTJ* 32 (1 June 1800–16 February 1801). Jeffer-

son writes, "I view great cities as pestilential to the morals, the health and the liberties of man. true, they nourish some of the elegant arts; but the useful ones can thrive elsewhere, and less perfection in the others with more health virtue & freedom would be my choice."

33. Nichols and Griswold, *Thomas Jefferson, Landscape Architect,* 38–75; Padover, *Thomas Jefferson and the National Capital.* Padover lists the "principal men in charge of the Capitol from 1793 to 1850" (519–22), including commissioners of the District of Columbia, building superintendents, commissioners of public buildings, architects, draftsmen, sculptors, and the superintendent of stonework and quarries, as well as men within the surveying department.

34. Nichols and Griswold, *Thomas Jefferson, Landscape Architect,* 38.

35. Library of Congress, *A Century of Lawmaking: United States Statutes at Large,* First Congress, Session II, vol. 1, chap. 28, Statue 2, 16 July 1790, 130. Although George Washington was certainly aware of many of the details concerning the planning of the federal city, he was not as directly involved as Jefferson.

36. TJ to Pierre Charles L'Enfant, 2 March 1791, *PTJ-D* (http://rotunda.upress.virginia.edu/founders/TSJN-01-19-02-0093); original source *PTJ* 19 (24 January–31 March 1791). L'Enfant was a Frenchman who came to America to fight in the Revolutionary War, initially on Lafayette's and later on General Washington's staff. For an elaborate discussion of L'Enfant's role in the development of Washington, D.C., see Berg, *Grand Avenues.* Although Jefferson is known to have drawn a small sketch plan (not shown) of the proposed federal city in early 1791, L'Enfant's original plan with future modifications by Ellicott was much more elaborate and in no way predicated on Jefferson's earlier work.

37. TJ to Pierre Charles L'Enfant, 17 March 1791, *PTJ-D* (http://rotunda.upress.virginia.edu/founders/TSJN-01-20-02-0001-0009); original source *PTJ* 20 (1 April–4 August 1791).

38. TJ to Pierre Charles L'Enfant, 10 April 1791, *PTJ-D* (http://rotunda.upress.virginia.edu/founders/TSJN-01-20-02-0001-0015); original source *PTJ* 20 (1 April–4 August 1791). It is not known precisely which maps of those named European cities Jefferson had collected, but based on his habits, it might be presumed that they were current and, overall, relatively inexpensive.

39. TJ to Pierre Charles L'Enfant, 27 February 1792, *PTJ-D* (http://rotunda.upress.virginia.edu/founders/TSJN-01-23-02-0153); original source *PTJ* 23 (January–31 May 1792).

40. Mathews, *Andrew Ellicott,* 71–88.

41. Padover, *Thomas Jefferson and the National Capital,* 463, 520. Latrobe was a multitalented British-born architect who immigrated to the United States in 1795. For a more extensive discussion of the role of Nicholas King, see Ehrenberg, "Nicholas King."

42. TJ, *Thomas Jefferson, Architect,* 13–17, 84–89; Nichols and Griswold, *Thomas Jefferson, Landscape Architect,* 90–125, 148–76. For a concise history, illustrated with many of Jefferson's studies for the university's buildings, see Wilson, *Thomas Jefferson's Academical Village.*

43. Edgerton, "Florentine Interest in Ptolemaic Cartography," 275, 290; Hurni and Sell, "Cartography and Architecture." The latter note the strong historical connection between cartography and architecture (330–31).

44. TJ to John Page, 21 February 1770, *PTJ-D* (http://rotunda.upress.virginia.edu/founders/TSJN-01-01-02-0023); original source *PTJ* 1 (1760–1776). The Shadwell plantation was Jefferson's birthplace, and only a short distance from Monticello.

45. TJ, *Garden Book,* 25–27.

46. Nichols and Griswold, *Thomas Jefferson, Landscape Architect,* xi.

47. TJ, *Garden Book* and *Farm Book.*

48. TJ, *Thomas Jefferson, Architect,* 26.

49. TJ to the Trustees of the Lottery for East Tennessee College, 6 May 1810, *PTJ-D* (http://rotunda.upress.virginia.edu/founders/TSJN -03-02-02-0322); original source *PTJ-R* 2 (16 November 1809–11 August 1810).

50. TJ, *Thomas Jefferson, Architect,* 80.

51. The most complete, published discussion of Jefferson's drawings is in TJ, *Thomas Jefferson, Architect.* The University of Virginia maintains a "Catalog of Jefferson Drawings" (http://www2 .iath.virginia.edu/wilson/catalogs/catalog .html), as well as a digital collection of those drawings, based on the Nichol's index (http:// iris.lib.virginia.edu/rmds/nichols/index.html).

2. *A Virginia Geography*

1. Brown, "Jefferson's Notes on Virginia," 467–73; Ferguson, "Mysterious Obligation," 381– 406; Ogburn, "Structure and Meaning," 141–50.

2. TJ, *Notes* (1972 ed.), xi.

3. Hayes, *Road to Monticello,* 233–59; Jackson, *Thomas Jefferson and the Stony Mountains,* 25–41; Malone, *Jefferson and His Time,* 1:373– 89; Peterson, *Thomas Jefferson,* 186–91. Malone observes that it was understandable that Jefferson should begin the replies with a geographical note, although Marbois had not specified the need to do so (377), and goes on to assert that Jefferson's work was the first such detailed description of an American state, and a major precursor to future state and federal reports on natural and human resources (379). Malone considered *Notes* the most important contemporary American scientific work.

4. Jackson, *Thomas Jefferson and the Stony Mountains,* 25. Jackson described the pioneering importance of the *Notes* and its importance to Jefferson's future role in the West. Although it was written in a highly personal style, and never intended as a formal academic treatise, there is little question that the *Notes* uses a geographic scaffolding for much of its discussion, and it is no accident that Jefferson begins his discussion with a cartographic statement of boundaries (Brückner, *Geographic Revolution,* 132–34), as so many of his political visions were rooted in geography (Lawson-Peebles, *Landscape and Written Expression,* 165–95). See also Pattison, "Four Traditions," 203. The *Notes* includes all four of his outlined geographical traditions: spatial, area studies, man-land, and earth-science.

5. Morse's *The American Geography; or, A View of the Present Situation of the United States of America* first appeared in 1789, although the shorter and less-focused work, *Geography Made Easy: Being a Short, but Comprehensive System of that very useful and agreeable Science,* was published in 1784.

6. In both the 1789 and 1792 editions of Morse's *The American Geography,* he devoted roughly forty pages (360–400) to the geography of Virginia, with more than 70 percent of the text quoted directly from Jefferson. Morse writes, "In the following description of Virginia, what is included between inverted commas, is taken from Mr. Jefferson's notes on Virginia, except in the instances where the reader is otherwise informed" (360).

7. Two lists of queries came from Marbois: one sixteen in number, and the other, twenty-two. It is not entirely clear which came first (i.e., whether the smaller list was expanded or the larger list condensed). This is discussed at length in Nancy Heywood, "A Draft Copy of the 'Notes on the State of Connecticut'" (http:// www.masshist.org/objects/2010april.php).

8. Hayes, *Road to Monticello,* 235.

9. Jackson, *Thomas Jefferson and the Stony*

Mountains, 26. Jefferson supposedly did not give up on the idea of a revised edition until 1814.

10. Mayhew, "Geography in Eighteenth-Century British Education," 732; Withers, "Eighteenth-Century Geography," 715–16. The subject of geography in the late eighteenth and early nineteenth centuries most commonly referred to what we now term "physical geography."

11. TJ, *Notes* (1972 ed.), 3–4. Jefferson references the work of "Cassini," who was Cassini I, or Giovanni Domenico (Jean Dominique) Cassini, the Italian-born astronomer and mathematician who moved to Paris in 1669. He also mostly references latitude, not longitude, in the bulk of his writings. This was because of contemporary uncertainties in measurements of the latter.

12. Ibid., 5–16.

13. Ibid., 17.

14. Ibid., 18–20.

15. Ibid., 21–25. Jefferson, in his manuscript notes, goes on to comment on other major cascades in North America; see 263–65.

16. Verner, "Maps and Plates," 32–33. Jefferson's personal copy of the *Notes,* part of the Tracy W. McGregor Collection of American History at the Albert and Shirley Small Special Collections Library of the University of Virginia, includes several sketches by Jefferson not seen in the original printings, among them the "Eye Draught of Mammoth Cave," "Plan of Madison's and Amen's Caverns," "Diagram of Siphon Spring," "Sketch of Several Ancient Fortifications," and "Sketch of the Forts on the Scioto River." These additional drawings were likely inserted with an eye toward a revised edition, which was never published.

17. TJ, *Notes* (1972 ed.), 26–72. Buffon was also a mathematician and cosmologist, and had several other associates involved in the production of his massive, 36-volume *Histoire Naturelle, Générale et Particulière,* a work that covered the animal and mineral "kingdoms of nature." For a more detailed discussion of Jefferson's contestations with Buffon, see Dugatkin's *Mr. Jefferson and the Giant Moose.* In spite of Jefferson's disagreement with Buffon's assessments, he included Buffon's *Natural History* in a 14 March 1818 letter to Nathaniel Burwell concerning book recommendations for "female education."

18. TJ, *Notes* (1972 ed.), 73.

19. Kendall, "America's First Great Global Warming Debate," 1–2. Webster did not approve of Jefferson's apparent sources, and accused him of relying on the opinions of the elderly and middle-aged. The major target of Webster's ire was Samuel Williams, author of the *The Natural and Civil History of Vermont* (1794), a book that Jefferson owned and referenced in the *Notes.*

20. TJ, *Notes* (1972 ed.), 82–87.

21. Ibid., 92–107. See 100–101 for the quote pertaining to the origin of the aboriginal inhabitants.

22. Ibid., 108.

23. Ibid., 110. The remark about "Christian people" also applies to the legal concept of the Right of Discovery, discussed further in chapter 6.

24. Verner, "Mr. Jefferson Makes a Map," 96–97. Actually, the translator for the French version of the *Notes,* Abbé Morellet, had suggested that the map might help sales, and Jefferson agreed.

25. Pedley, *Commerce of Cartography,* 186–87.

26. Verner, "Mr. Jefferson Makes a Map," 102–5.

27. Ibid., 96–99.

28. J. H. Pratt, "American Prime Meridians," 237–40.

29. Verner, "Mr. Jefferson Makes a Map," 97.

30. Ibid., 98. The first state of the Fry-Jefferson map, with a printed date of 1751, was entitled "A Map of the Inhabited Part of Virginia," with the phrasing slightly changed for subsequent states. Jefferson likely used a later

version, given his penchant for up-to-date information, very possibly a circa 1776 variant that appeared in Jefferys's *The American Atlas,* which was published posthumously by Robert Sayer and John Bennett. For a discussion of the various states of the English version of the map, see Verner, "Fry and Jefferson Map," 83–89.

31. Verner, "Mr. Jefferson Makes a Map," 97. Hutchins's map had been prepared as a companion to his text, *A Topographical Description of Virginia, Pennsylvania, Maryland, and North Carolina, Comprehending the Rivers Ohio, Kenhawa, Sioto, Cherokee, Wabash, Illiniois, Missisippi &c.* (London, 1778).

32. Verner, "Mr. Jefferson Makes a Map," 98.

33. Ibid., 98n15: "Manuscript fragment, M Hi. See also an additional fragment headed 'Materials for improving the map of Virginia' which is essentially the same but probably noted at a later date."

34. TJ to Francis Hopkinson, 14 August 1786, *PTJ-D* (http://rotunda.upress.virginia.edu/founders/TSJN-01-10-02-0166); original source *PTJ* 10 (22 June–31 December 1786). See also Verner, "Mr. Jefferson Makes a Map," 98–99.

3. Library of the Geography of America

1. Jefferson's most commonly cited quote extolling books and reading came from a 10 June 1815 letter to John Adams: "I cannot live without books: but fewer will suffice where amusement, and not use, is the only future object." For a more general discussion see D. L. Wilson, *Jefferson's Books.*

2. TJ to Samuel H. Smith, 21 September 1814, *PTJ-R* 7:681–82. The actual number of books was likely about six thousand.

3. TJ to Abraham Baldwin, 14 April 1802, ME 19:128–29.

4. Kraus, "Private Libraries," 38–40. Books were not included in Mather's estate inventory,

although his son Samuel wrote, "My Father's Library was by far the most valuable part of the family Property. It consisted of 7,000 or 8,000 Volumes of the most curious and chosen Authors, and a prodigious Number of valuable Manuscripts, which had been collected by my Ancestors for five Generations" (39).

5. D. L. Wilson, *Jefferson's Books,* 12–13, 53n4.

6. "The John Adams Library at the Boston Public Library." Although Adams had a number of holdings related to geography and cartography, they did not come close in breadth or depth to those of Jefferson. Nonetheless, Adams was certainly aware of the contemporary importance of the subject of geography.

7. Smart, "Private Libraries," 39–40.

8. Sowerby, *Catalog of the Library of Thomas Jefferson,* vol. 4; chapter 29 is devoted to geography and chapter 30 to architecture. Subdividing the geography section, Jefferson had 26 entries under general geography, 62 for Europe, 24 for Asia, 13 for Africa, and 174 for America. Although there are limitations in relying on Sowerby's researches, the catalog still gives a reasonable idea of the holdings and the intellectual arenas covered. Sowerby did not follow Jefferson's own classification scheme; for discussions of the pros and cons of the Sowerby catalog, see D. L. Wilson, "Sowerby Revisited," 615–28, and Gilreath, "Sowerby Revirescent and Revised," 219–32.

9. D. L. Wilson, *Jefferson's Books,* 15. A list of books and maps in Peter Jefferson's library can be found in "Books in Colonial Virginia," *Virginia Magazine of History and Biography* 10 (1903): 391.

10. Jefferson's 1783 classification can be found at http://www.masshist.org/thomasjeffersonpapers/catalog1783/catalog1783_chapters.html.

11. This is no surprise, given the expansive

nature of geography, which was not yet a widely recognized, formal academic specialization in Jefferson's time (see Withers, "Eighteenth-Century Geography," 717–22; and Mayhew, "Geography in Eighteenth-Century British Education," 731–33).

12. Gilreath and Wilson, *Thomas Jefferson's Library,* 7. This observation is predicated on the 1823 Trist list, presumably based on Jefferson's own 1812 catalog, which has not been found but had accompanied the books that went to the Library of Congress in 1815.

13. An evolving compilation of various transcribed lists and catalogs relating to Jefferson's books can be found in "Thomas Jefferson's Libraries." A discussion of his various libraries—including those developed at Shadwell, Monticello pre- and post-retirement, and Poplar Forest—is posted on Library Thing at http://www.library thing.com/profile/ThomasJefferson.

14. These practices can be verified by scanning *Jefferson's Memorandum Books.*

15. These listings are predicated on Jefferson's own classification, as they appear in Gilreath and Wilson (see note 12 above; accessible at http://catdir.loc.gov/catdir/toc/becites/main/ jefferson/88607928_ch29.html). The numbers that actually appear by the Gilreath and Wilson listings refer to those in Sowerby's *Catalog of the Library of Thomas Jefferson.* More precise title detail can then be obtained by searching via "Thomas Jefferson's Libraries."

16. Some of these varied works are discussed further in Jackson, *Thomas Jefferson and the Stony Mountains,* 86–97. Although Jefferson perhaps valued the content of the works of Theodore de Bry on some levels, he was skeptical of their overall veracity. In a letter to John Adams dated 11 June 1812, concerning Native American traditions (*PTJ-D,* http://rotunda.upress. virginia.edu/founders/TSJN-03-05-02-0100;

original source *PTJ-R* 5 [1 May 1812–10 March 1813]), he wrote: "The scope of your enquiry would scarcely, I suppose, take in the three folio volumes of Latin by De Bry. In these fact and fable are mingled together, without regard to any favorite system. They are less suspicious therefore in their complexion, more original and authentic, than those of Lafitau and Adair. This is a work of great curiosity, extremely rare, so as never to be bought in Europe, but on the breaking up, and selling some antient library. On one of these occasions a bookseller procured me a copy, which, unless you have one, is probably the only one in America."

4. Jefferson as Expedition Planner

1. Ronda, "To Acquire What Knolege You Can." He emphasizes the importance of preliminary mission-planning prior to the physical launch of an expedition and the importance of carefully posed questions during its course (409–10). Jefferson's formal, preliminary written instructions were typical of the time, and England's Royal Society had provided many types of travel lists of increasingly practical questions for fifty years. In addition, some of the great mapmakers of the European Enlightenment, including England's Aaron Arrowsmith and France's Jean Baptiste Bourguignon d'Anville, worked from their offices, and hence were compilers, not field surveyors.

2. Jefferson owned a later edition (1802) of this work (*Voyages from Montreal, on the river St. Laurence, through the continent of North America, to the frozen and Pacific oceans: in the years 1789 and 1793: with a preliminary account of the rise, progress and present state of the fur trade of that country*), and his copy was part of the collection donated in 1815 to form the basis for the new Library of Congress. For a discussion of the impact of Mackenzie's writings on Jefferson, see Ronda,

"Dreams and Discoveries" (149), and Jackson, *Thomas Jefferson and the Stony Mountains* (121–24). Mackenzie's 1801 *A Map of America* was carried by Lewis and Clark on their expedition.

3. D. Allen, "Acquiring 'Knowledge of Our Own Continent,'" 209–11.

4. J. L. Allen, *Lewis and Clark and the Image of the American Northwest,* xix–xxvi.

5. TJ to General Clark, 4 December 1783, *PTJ-D* (http://rotunda.upress.virginia.edu/founders/TSJN-01-06-02-0289); original source *PTJ* 6 (21 May 1781–1 March 1784).

6. General Clark to TJ, 8 February 1784, *PTJ-D* (http://rotunda.upress.virginia.edu/founders/TSJN-01-15-02-0587); original source *PTJ* 15 (27 March 1789–30 November 1789).

7. See Ledyard, *Journey,* 3–31, for Watrous's concise biographical sketch of the explorer. See also Jackson, *Thomas Jefferson and The Stony Mountains,* 45–56, which discusses the writings of Jean-François de Galaup, Comte de Lapérouse, another member of Cook's third voyage. Jefferson was aware of the writings of both men. A copy of Ledyard's published journals was part of the 1815 donation to the Library of Congress.

8. TJ to Reverend (Bishop) James Madison, 19 July 1788, *PTJ-D* (http://rotunda.upress. virginia.edu/founders/TSJN-01-13-02-0280); original source *PTJ* 13 (March–7 October 1788).

9. TJ to John Jay, 14 August 1785, *PTJ-D* (http://rotunda.upress.virginia.edu/founders/TSJN-01-08-02-0298); original source *PTJ* 8 (25 February–31 October 1785). See also note 7 above concerning Lapérouse.

10. TJ to Mr. Andrew Michaud [*sic*], ca. 30 April 1793, *PTJ-D* (http://rotunda.upress. virginia.edu/founders/TSJN-01-25-02-0569); original source *PTJ* 25 (1 January–10 May 1793). For a general description of the planning of the Michaux expedition, see Jackson, *Thomas Jefferson and the Stony Mountains,* 74–78.

11. C. Williams, "Explorer, Botanist, Courier, or Spy?" 98–106.

12. J. L. Allen, *Lewis and Clark and the Image of the American Northwest,* 61–62. Allen goes on to discuss Jefferson's diffuse scientific and geographic communications, which convinced him of the existence of the "Passage to India" that might be found via the Missouri River and its watershed (62).

13. Don Higginbotham, "Military Education before West Point," and Watson, "Developing 'Republican Machines,'" in McDonald, *Thomas Jefferson's Military Academy,* 43–45 and 155–57, respectively.

14. Jackson, *Letters of the Lewis and Clark Expedition,* 1:12–13. The $2,500 request was based on Lewis's itemized estimate of the expeditionary costs (see 8–9). Jackson speculates, in a note on page 9, that Jefferson and Lewis were, for political reasons, underestimating the projected costs of the expedition.

15. J. L. Allen, *Lewis and Clark and the Image of the American Northwest,* 73–108. Allen's concise discussion of the preparation for the expedition is remarkable. Many of the maps mentioned are illustrated in other chapters herein.

16. Gallatin to TJ, 14 March 1803, in Jackson, *Letters of the Lewis and Clark Expedition,* 1:27–28. Other than Gallatin, very few of Jefferson's contemporaries could communicate with him in detail regarding these specific cartographic issues.

17. TJ to Gallatin, 20 March 1803, ibid., 1:31–32.

18. Gallatin to TJ, 13 April 1803, ibid., 1:132–34.

19. TJ to Lewis, 20 June 1803, ibid., 1:61–66. Due to the length and detail of the instructions, the quote here is only a small portion of the document.

20. Perhaps the most focused, published dis-

cussion of the maps used in planning the expedition is John Logan Allen's *Lewis and Clark and the Image of the American Northwest,* 76–103. Nicholas King eventually became surveyor of the city of Washington, in addition to his work on the base and expedition maps of the Lewis and Clark expedition (see entry in *Tooley's Dictionary of Mapmakers,* 3:28, and Ehrenberg, "Nicholas King," 31–65).

21. Aaron Arrowsmith was originally a land surveyor, and eventually became hydrographer to the Prince of Wales (ca. 1810) and then King George IV (1820). See *Tooley's Dictionary of Mapmakers,* 1:47–48, and Elizabeth Baigent's entry in the online edition of the *Oxford Dictionary of National Biography* (subscription access at http://www.oxforddnb.com/).

22. As with most of the mapmakers discussed in this section, biographical entries are available in *Tooley's Dictionary of Mapmakers.* For a discussion of Delisle's landmark image of the Mississippi River, see Alfred E. Lemmon, "La Louisiane/La Luisiana: A Bourbon Country," in Lemmon, Macgill, and Wiese, *Charting Louisiana: Five Hundred Years of Maps,* map 18, 58, and Wheat, *Mapping the Transmississippi West,* 1:66–67.

23. There are many editions/variants of the Mitchell map; see the detailed discussion by Matthew Edney at http://www.oshermaps.org/exhibitions/map-commentaries/most-important-map-us-history. See also Edney's "Publishing History of John Mitchell's 1755 Map."

24. Jackson, *Letters of the Lewis and Clark Expedition;* Lewis and Clark, *Journals of the Lewis and Clark Expedition.* Another very useful resource is "Envisaging the West: Thomas Jefferson and the Roots of Lewis and Clark," which includes transcriptions of primary source documents and is illustrated with high-resolution,

maneuverable map images contemporary with the time of the planned expedition.

25. Library of Congress, Geography and Map Division, "Louisiana: European Explorations and the Louisiana Purchase" (see pages 54–66 of the pdf essay at http://memory.loc.gov/ammem/collections/maps/lapurchase/lapurchase.pdf). TJ to Lewis, 16 November 1803, in Jackson, *Letters of the Lewis and Clark Expedition,* 1:136–38. The resulting treaty was ratified in the U.S. Senate on 20 October 1803. With respect to the Right of Discovery as applicable to the purchase, see R. J. Miller, *Native America,* 71–72.

26. Jefferson and Dunbar, *Documents Relating to the Purchase and Exploration of Louisiana,* 11–45. The original manuscripts, both for Jefferson's overview of the territorial history and Dunbar's "The Exploration of the Red, the Black, and the Washita Rivers," are held by the Library of the American Philosophical Society.

27. Ibid., 11–18. Jefferson references books within his own library, including works by Michel Guillaume St. Jean de Crèvecoeur, Louis Hennepin, Thomas Jefferys, Henri Joutel, Dumont de Montigny, Antoine-Simon Le Page du Pratz, Guillaume Thomas Francois Raynal, and William Russell.

28. Ibid., 18–21.

29. Ibid., 23–24.

30. Ibid., 27.

31. Ibid., 27n. Jefferson is referring to maps by the British mapmaker and publisher Herman Moll, the eminent French cartographer Guillaume Delisle (the 1718 French map referenced is almost certainly Carte de la Louisiane), and the German mapmaker and publisher Johann Baptist Homann (including the heirs to his publishing house).

32. Ibid., 40–41.

33. Jefferson was knowledgeable about Pike's expedition and the varied sorts of geographic

and cartographic information it generated. Pike's 1810 published report, *An Account of Expeditions to the Sources of the Mississippi,* was part of the library Jefferson sold to Congress in 1815. For a general discussion of Jefferson's involvement in the Dunbar-Hunter expedition, see the introduction to Berry, Beasley, and Clements, *The Forgotten Expedition,* xi–xxxvi. For a similar discussion of Jefferson's involvement with the Freeman-Custis expedition, see the two prefaces to Flores, *Southern Counterpart to Lewis and Clark,* ix–xvi and xvii–xx, and the introduction, 3–90.

34. Berry, "Expedition of William Dunbar and George Hunter," 386–87, 391. George Hunter was a Philadelphia businessman, chemist, and explorer. The Ouachita River runs through Arkansas and Louisiana, emptying into the Red River just before it joins the Mississippi River. The Ouachita is labeled as "Washita" in Arrowsmith's 1802 *Map of the United States of North America.* The expedition had been deemed the "Grand Expedition," but it was ultimately cut short due to various physical obstacles, including the winter weather (Berry, Beasley, and Clements, *The Forgotten Expedition,* xii, xxix).

35. TJ to William Dunbar, 13 March 1804, in "Envisaging the West" (http://jeffersonswest .unl.edu/archive/view_doc.php?id=jef.00118). By this time, Jefferson had been communicating with Dunbar for several years.

36. A high-resolution image of King's map appears in the American Memory Map Collection (http://hdl.loc.gov/loc.gmd/g40020.ct001324). Although the cataloging entry indicates 1804 as the publication date, there are good reasons to suspect that this was actually published in 1806, with copies sometimes appearing in Jefferson's presidential message (see note 37).

37. TJ, *Message from the President of the United States.*

38. Flores, *Southern Counterpart to Lewis and*

Clark, 320–25, reproduces the full text of this letter, with an accompanying editorial note on page 319.

39. Ibid., 18–19. Several copies of that map appear to have been made, one of which was given to Albert Gallatin. Note that Jefferson's impression, and that of other educated contemporary analysts, was incorrect; had the full length of the river been explored, they never would have ended up near Santa Fe in the southern Rockies.

40. Ibid., xi.

41. A high-resolution copy of this image appears in the American Memory Map Collection (http://hdl.loc.gov/loc.gmd/g3992r.ct000689).

5. A Geography of Letters

1. See the introduction to Stanford University's "Mapping the Republic of Letters" (https:// republicofletters.stanford.edu/).

2. Christoph Daniel Ebeling to TJ, 30 July 1795, *PTJ-D* (http://rotunda.upress.virginia.edu/ founders/TSJN-01-28-02-0331); original source *PTJ* 28 (1 January 1794–29 February 1796). "Mr. Morse" refers to Jedidiah Morse, sometimes called the "Father of American Geography."

3. See "U.S. Teen Mobile Report: Calling Yesterday, Texting Today, Using Apps Tomorrow," *Nielsen News Online,* 14 October 2010 (http://www.switched.com/2010/10/14/the -average-teen-sends-over-3-000-texts-a-month -nielsen-finds/).

4. By my count, looking through the online papers accessible via the American Founding Era collection of Rotunda (http://rotunda.upress .virginia.edu/, the digital imprint of the University of Virginia Press), Jefferson's written output was roughly four times that of Adams.

5. There is an extensive literature discussing the importance of land and varied notions of landscape in America. A few examples include J. L. Allen, *Lewis and Clark and the Image of the*

American Northwest, xix–xxvi and 1–47; Cosgrove, *Geography and Vision,* 85–118; Casey, *Representing Place,* xiii–xviii, 3–19, and 213–30; and Price, *Dividing the Land.*

6. TJ to Alexander White, 19 April 1769, *PTJ-D* (http://rotunda.upress.virginia.edu/founders/TSJN-01-01-02-0017); original source *PTJ* 1 (1760–1776).

7. Perkins, Buchanan & Brown to TJ, 2 October 1769, *PTJ-D* (http://rotunda.upress.virginia.edu/founders/TSJN-01-01-02-0022); original source *PTJ* 1 (1760–1776). Petty was a mid-seventeenth-century polymath (scientist, philosopher, economist, physician) who was well known for his contributions to cartography and surveying, including the Down Survey of Ireland. Additional background material can be found at http://socserv2.socsci.mcmaster.ca/~econ/ugcm/3ll3/petty/index.html.

8. TJ to Horatio Gates, 4 October 1780, *PTJ-D* (http://rotunda.upress.virginia.edu/founders/TSJN-01-04-02-0012); original source *PTJ* 4 (1 October 1780–24 February 1781). Colonel Senf was a military engineer and director for the development of the Santee Canal, one of the earliest canals built in the United States.

9. TJ to Lafayette, 8 March 1781, *PTJ-D* (http://rotunda.upress.virginia.edu/founders/TSJN-01-05-02-0120); original source *PTJ* 5 (25 February 1781–20 May 1781). Marie-Joseph Paul Yves Roch Gilbert du Motier, Marquis de Lafayette, was not himself a mapmaker, but he did employ one of the most skillful cartographers of the American Revolutionary War era, Michel Capitaine du Chesnoy. Although there is no evidence of direct contact between Jefferson and Capitaine du Chesnoy, the cartographer had been in contact with General Washington. Jefferson and Lafayette were long-time correspondents, and Lafayette eventually stayed at Monticello in 1824.

10. TJ to Lafayette, 14 March 1781, *PTJ-D* (http://rotunda.upress.virginia.edu/founders/TSJN-01-05-02-0190); original source *PTJ* 5 (25 February 1781–20 May 1781).

11. None of the other colonial governors responded with Jefferson's measure of detail. For a list of Marbois's original queries, see his document dated before 30 November 1780, *PTJ-D* (http://rotunda.upress.virginia.edu/founders/TSJN-01-04-02-0197); original source *PTJ* 4 (1 October 1780–24 February 1781). Jefferson's *Notes* is discussed in greater detail in chapter 2.

12. TJ to Thomas Hutchins, 24 January 1784, *PTJ-D* (http://rotunda.upress.virginia.edu/founders/TSJN-01-27-02-0673); original source *PTJ* 27 (1 September-31 December 1793). See Hoffman, "Queries Regarding the Western Rivers," 15–28, regarding the possible intent of Jefferson's letter to Hutchins.

13. TJ to James Madison, 20 February 1784, *PTJ-D* (http://rotunda.upress.virginia.edu/founders/TSJN-01-06-02-0406); original source *PTJ* 6 (21 May 1781–1 March 1784).

14. James Madison to TJ, 9 January 1785, *PTJ-D* (http://rotunda.upress.virginia.edu/founders/TSJN-01-07-02-0433); original source *PTJ* 7 (2 March 1784–25 February 1785).

15. TJ to General George Rogers Clark, 29 January 1780, *PTJ-D* (http://rotunda.upress.virginia.edu/founders/TSJN-01-03-02-0311); original source *PTJ* 3 (18 June 1779–30 September 1780). See chapter 6 for a discussion of the importance of settlements at the mouths of rivers in terms of the legal implications of the Right of Discovery.

16. TJ to General Clark, 26 November 1782, *PTJ-D* (http://rotunda.upress.virginia.edu/founders/TSJN-01-06-02-0193); original source *PTJ* 6 (21 May 1781–1 March 1784).

17. TJ to General Clark, 4 December 1783, *PTJ-D* (http://rotunda.upress.virginia.edu/found

ers/TSJN-01-06-02-0289); original source *PTJ* 6 (21 May 1781–1 March 1784).

18. General Clark to TJ, 8 February 1784, *PTJ-D* (http://rotunda.upress.virginia.edu/founders/TSJN-01-15-02-0587); original source *PTJ* 15 (27 March 1789–30 November 1789).

19. David Rittenhouse to TJ, 14 April 1787, *PTJ-D* (http://rotunda.upress.virginia.edu/founders/TSJN-01-11-02-0281); original source *PTJ* 11 (1 January–6 August 1787).

20. John Churchman to TJ, 6 June 1787, *PTJ-D* (http://rotunda.upress.virginia.edu/founders/TSJN-01-11-02-0378); original source *PTJ* 11 (1 January–6 August 1787). The accurate determination of longitude was an ongoing problem for navigators and mapmakers, and Churchman knew Jefferson would understand his remarks. A major portion of these difficulties related to accurate measurement of time over long distances. Jefferson did not have access to John Harrison's remarkable chronometer, and he spent years attempting to develop an American method for calculating longitude (see "Longitude," *Thomas Jefferson Encyclopedia,* http://www.monticell.org/site/research-and-collections/longitude). On 24 June 1812 Jefferson wrote to Andrew Ellicott, "A great deal is yet wanting to ascertain the true geography of our country; more indeed as to it's longitudes than latitudes"; *PTJ-D* (http://rotunda.upress.virginia.edu/founders/TSJN-03-05-02-0137); original source *PTJ-R* 5 (1 May 1812–10 March 1813)

21. For a detailed discussion of L'Enfant's involvement with the early design of Washington, D.C., see Berg, *Grand Avenues.*

22. TJ to Pierre Charles L'Enfant, [2] March 1791, *PTJ-D* (http://rotunda.upress.virginia.edu/founders/TSJN-01-19-02-0093); original source *PTJ* 19 (24 January–31 March 1791).

23. Pierre Charles L'Enfant to TJ, 11 March 1791, *PTJ-D* (http://rotunda.upress.virginia.edu/

founders/TSJN-01-20-02-0001-0004); original source *PTJ* 20 (1 April–4 August 1791).

24. TJ to Pierre Charles L'Enfant, 17 March 1791, *PTJ-D* (http://rotunda.upress.virginia.edu/founders/TSJN-01-20-02-0001-0009); original source PTJ 20 (1 April–4 August 1791). The postscript was not in the original draft; it was added after consultation with President Washington.

25. TJ to Pierre Charles L'Enfant, 18 August 1791, *PTJ-D* (http://rotunda.upress.virginia.edu/founders/TSJN-01-22-02-0047); original source PTJ 22 (6 August 1791–31 December 1791). The letter discussing Jefferson's European town plans, along with additional instructions for L'Enfant's project, was a bit earlier, on 10 April 1791; *PTJ-D* (http://rotunda.upress.virginia.edu/founders/TSJN-01-20-02-0001-0015); original source *PTJ* 20 (1 April–4 August 1791).

26. For details of Ellicott's life and extensive involvement in surveying projects of vital concern to the history of the early republic, see Mathews, *Andrew Ellicott.*

27. TJ (as secretary of state) to Andrew Ellicott, 2 February 1791, *PTJ-D* (http://rotunda.upress.virginia.edu/founders/TSJN-01-19-02-0001-0013); original source *PTJ* 19 (24 January–31 March 1791). Apparently the original manuscript letter has not been located, and the text supplied has been cited from Alexander, "A Sketch in the Life of Major Andrew Ellicott," 170–71.

28. Andrew Ellicott to TJ, 13 April 1801, *PTJ-D* (http://rotunda.upress.virginia.edu/founders/TSJN-01-33-02-0504); original source *PTJ* 33 (17 February–30 April 1801).

29. Jackson, *Letters of the Lewis and Clark Expedition,* 1:23–25.

30. Jackson, *Letters of the Lewis and Clark Expedition,* vols. 1 and 2. Jackson's index, in volume 2, contains nearly a full page of entries re-

garding letters to and from Jefferson pertaining to the expedition.

31. TJ to William Dunbar, 24 June 1799, *PTJ-D* (http://rotunda.upress.virginia.edu/founders/TSJN-01-31-02-0120); original source *PTJ* 31 (1 February 1799–31 May 1800). Dunbar was a university-educated Scottish immigrant who had been hired by the Spanish government in 1798 to survey the boundary between the United States and Spanish West Florida. On Jefferson's recommendation, he had been elected to the American Philosophical Society in 1800.

32. William Dunbar to TJ, 4 [i.e., 6] October 1799, *PTJ-D* (http://rotunda.upress.virginia.edu/founders/TSJN-01-31-02-0170); original source *PTJ* 31 (1 February 1799–31 May 1800).

33. TJ to William Dunbar, 12 January 1801, *PTJ-D* (http://rotunda.upress.virginia.edu/founders/TSJN-01-32-02-0322); original source *PTJ* 32 (1 June 1800–16 February 1801).

34. TJ to Volney, 8 January 1797, *PTJ-D* (http://rotunda.upress.virginia.edu/founders/TSJN-01-29-02-0202); original source *PTJ* 29 (1 March 1796–31 December 1797). Jefferson recorded various meteorological observations in his writings, including in his *Memorandum Books* and *Notes.*

35. For a detailed discussion of Humboldt and Jefferson's friendship, see Rebok, *Humboldt and Jefferson.*

36. TJ to von Humboldt, 6 December 1813, FE 10:430. The correspondence of these two Enlightenment giants has been the subject of several academic discussions; see Rebok, "Enlightened Correspondents" and *Humboldt and Jefferson* (which reproduces their letters in an appendix, on pages 143–59), and Terra, "Alexander von Humboldt's Correspondence." Jefferson's comments in the cited sections pertaining to the apparent plagiarisms of Aaron Arrowsmith and Zebulon Pike were in direct response to an ear-lier complaint from Humboldt—see von Humboldt to TJ, 20 December 1811, *PTJ-D* (http://rotunda.upress.virginia.edu/founders/TSJN-03-04-02-0270); original source *PTJ-R* 4 (18 June 1811–30 April 1812).

37. Bishop James Madison was named the eighth president of the College of William and Mary in 1777, and was consecrated the first Episcopal bishop of the Diocese of Virginia in 1790. He understood the importance of mapmaking, and through his position at William and Mary was involved in the approval of licensure for state surveyors. Although cartography was not his personal work, he was instrumental in arranging the production of the first map of Virginia compiled, engraved, and published in the commonwealth in 1807, and hence this map, *A Map of Virginia Formed from Actual Surveys,* is often called the "Bishop Madison" map. See Stephenson and McKee, *Virginia in Maps,* 120–21 and 139–45, and Wooldridge, *Mapping Virginia,* 199–205, 358. The Bishop Madison map is reproduced, with a brief accompanying discussion, in chapter 7.

38. TJ to Bishop James Madison, 4 March 1798, *PTJ-D* (http://rotunda.upress.virginia.edu/founders/TSJN-01-30-02-0104); original source *PTJ* 30 (1 January 1798–31 January 1799). A number of phrases in this letter are illegible, as indicated by the bracketed ellipses. An extensive, associated note discusses individuals and places remarked on therein, including Franz Xaver von Zach, a respected German astronomer, and the by-then world-renowned observatory at Lilienthal overseen by Johann Hieronymus Schröter.

39. Bishop Madison to TJ, 13 March 1798, *PTJ-D* (http://rotunda.upress.virginia.edu/founders/TSJN-01-30-02-0119); original source *PTJ* 30 (1 January 1798–31 January 1799).

40. TJ to Bishop Madison, 29 December 1811, *PTJ-D* (http://rotunda.upress.virginia.edu/

founders/TSJN-03-04-02-0283); original source *PTJ-R* 4 (18 June 1811–30 April 1812). The map mentioned in this letter is the "Bishop Madison" map cited in note 37, above. A revised and updated version of that map was eventually published in 1818 after Madison's death.

41. *Tooley's Dictionary of Mapmakers,* 3:234. Ristow, *American Maps and Mapmakers,* 110–15. Ristow describes Melish as "one of the most energetic and competent commercial map publishers of his day."

42. John Melish to TJ, 18 January 1812, *PTJ-D* (http://rotunda.upress.virginia.edu/founders/TSJN-03-04-02-0331); original source *PTJ-R* 4 (18 June 1811–30 April 1812). A copy of this work was part of Jefferson's Great Library, which became the foundation of the Library of Congress.

43. TJ to John Melish, 13 January 1813, *PTJ-D* (http://rotunda.upress.virginia.edu/founders/TSJN-03-05-02-0478); original source *PTJ-R* 5 (1 May 1812–10 March 1813).

44. TJ to John Melish, 31 December 1816, ME 15:93. This letter is from the section entitled "Letters Written After His Return to the United States, 1789–1826."

6. Foreshadowing Manifest Destiny

1. See, for example, Drake, *Nation's Nature,* 230–59. See also Wallace, *Jefferson and the Indians,* and Mapp, *Elusive West.*

2. See Stephanson, *Manifest Destiny;* Weeks, *Building the Continental Empire;* and Weinberg, *Manifest Destiny.*

3. Staloff, *Hamilton, Adams, Jefferson,* introduction and chapter 3; Rebok, "Enlightened Correspondents."

4. Schöpflin and Hosking, *Myths and Nationhood.*

5. Dion, "Natural Law and Manifest Des-

tiny"; Meinig, *Atlantic America, 1492–1800,* 3–76.

6. Weeks, *Building the Continental Empire,* 61.

7. J. W. Pratt, "Origin of 'Manifest Destiny,'" 795–98. O'Sullivan, "Annexation," 5.

8. Greenberg, *Manifest Manhood,* 225.

9. Dion, "Natural Law and Manifest Destiny," 244.

10. Ibid., 243.

11. Owsley and Smith, *Filibusters and Expansionists,* 7–31 and 181–92.

12. TJ to Archibald Stuart, 25 January 1786, *PTJ-D* (http://rotunda.upress.virginia.edu/founders/TSJN-01-09-02-0192); original source *PTJ* 9 (1 November 1785–22 June 1786).

13. TJ's First Inaugural Address, 4 March 1801, *PTJ-D* (http://rotunda.upress.virginia.edu/founders/TSJN-01-33-02-0116-0004); original source *PTJ* 33 (17 February–30 April 1801).

14. Banning, *Liberty and Order;* TJ to John C. Breckinridge, 12 August 1803 (http://oll.libertyfund.org/?option=com_staticxt&staticfile=show.php%3Ftitle=875&chapter=64022&layout=html&Itemid=27).

15. TJ to John Jacob Astor, 24 May 1812, *PTJ-D* (http://rotunda.upress.virginia.edu/founders/TSJN-03-05-02-0056); original source *PTJ-R* 5 (28 November 1813–30 September 1814).

16. Kellner, *Alexander von Humboldt,* 62.

17. TJ to Alexander von Humboldt, 6 December 1813, *PTJ-D* (http://rotunda.upress.virginia.edu/founders/TSJN-03-07-02-0011); original source *PTJ-R* 7 (1 May 1812–10 March 1813).

18. Stephanson, *Manifest Destiny,* 3–27; Cherry, *God's New Israel,* 1–162; Scott, "Religious Origins of Manifest Destiny."

19. Dion, "Natural Law and Manifest Destiny," 228–31; Salisbury, "Red Puritans," 27–54; Bercovitch, *American Jeremiad.*

20. TJ to James Monroe, 17 June 1785, *PTJ-D*

(http://rotunda.upress.virginia.edu/founders/ TSJN-01-08-02-0174); original source *PTJ* 8 (25 February–31 October 1785).

21. TJ's First Inaugural Address, 4 March 1801, *PTJ-D*.

22. TJ to James Madison, 27 April 1809, *PTJ-D* (http://rotunda.upress.virginia.edu/found ers/TSJN-03-01-02-0140); original source *PTJ-R* 1 (4 March 1809–15 November 1809).

23. R. J. Miller, *Native America,* 50–53. When I use the word "Discovery" in this chapter's text—that is, with a capital "D"—I am referring to the legal principles of the Right of Discovery; lowercased "discovery" refers to an initial territorial find, involving the general idea of first exploration.

24. Ibid., 13–23.

25. Ibid., 59–76.

26. Ibid., 3–5, 76–103.

27. Ibid., 4.

28. Ibid., 4.

29. Ibid., 60–61.

30. TJ's "Opinion on Certain Georgia Land Grants," 3 May 1790, *PTJ-D* (http://rotunda. upress.virginia.edu/founders/TSJN-01-16-02 -0233); original source *PTJ* 16 (30 November 1789–4 July 1790).

31. R. J. Miller, *Native America,* 61–76.

32. M. Murphy, "Natural Law Tradition in Ethics"; Strauss, *Natural Right and History.*

33. Dion, "Natural Law and Manifest Destiny," 231–32.

34. TJ to Samuel Latham Mitchill, 13 June 1800, *PTJ-D* (http://rotunda.upress.virginia.edu/ founders/TSJN-01-32-02-0011) original source *PTJ* 32 (1 June 1800–16 February 1801).

35. TJ to Doctor John Manners, 12 June 1817, ME 15:124–26.

36. Meinig, *Continental America, 1800–1867,* 4–23; Kukla, *A Wilderness So Immense;* Geography and Map Division, Library of Congress,

"Louisiana: European Explorations and the Louisiana Purchase" (see the pdf file at http:// memory.loc.gov/ammem/collections/maps/ lapurchase/lapurchase.pdf, which runs to 118 pages and corresponds to the online exhibit and essay).

37. R. J. Miller, *Native America,* 71–72.

38. Geography and Map Division, Library of Congress, "Louisiana," 6. See also chapter 4 for a more detailed discussion of the varied maps Jefferson used in planning for the Lewis and Clark expedition.

39. Stein, *Worlds of Thomas Jefferson,* 382–94.

40. Jackson, *Thomas Jefferson and the Stony Mountains,* 104, 115n21.

41. TJ, "Queries as to Louisiana," FE 10:17–19. The dating of Jefferson's original seventeen queries is approximate, and is listed as 15 June 1803 (http://oll.libertyfund.org/title/806/87432).

42. TJ, "Account of Louisiana," 14 November 1803, *American State Papers: Miscellaneous,* vol. 1, 344; Document No. 164, 1st Session, 8th Congress (http://memory.loc.gov/cgi-bin/ ampage?collId=llsp&fileName=037/llsp037 .db&recNum=4).

43. TJ, "Limits and Bounds of Louisiana," in Jefferson and Dunbar, *Documents Relating to the Purchase and Exploration of Louisiana,* 27. It is not clear exactly which of Moll's and Homann's maps he was referencing, but three reasonable candidates include Herman Moll's *A Map of the West-Indies &c., Mexico or New Spain* (ca. 1736, http://www.davidrumsey.com/detail?id=1-1 -3762-430098&name=Map+of+the+West -Indies,+Mexico+or+New+Spain); Moll's *A New Map of the North Parts of America claimed by France under ye Names of Louisiana* (ca. 1720, http://hdl.loc.gov/loc.gmd/g3300.ct000677); and Johann Baptist Homann's ca. 1719 *Amplissimae Regionis Mississipi Seu Provinciae Ludovicianae à R. P. Ludovico Hennepin Francisc Miss*

in America Septentrionali (ca. 1719, http://con tent.lib.washington.edu/cdm4/item_viewer .php?CISOROOT=/maps&CISOPTR=154).

44. Stephanson, *Manifest Destiny,* 99–114; Cutright, *Lewis and Clark,* 1–29.

45. J. L. Allen, *Lewis and Clark and the Image of the American Northwest,* xix–xxvi and 1–48; G. Williams, *Voyages of Delusion.*

46. TJ, "Jefferson's Instructions to Lewis," in Jackson, *Letters of the Lewis and Clark Expedition,* 1:61–66.

47. See, for example, Jackson, *Letters of the Lewis and Clark Expedition;* Lewis and Clark, *Journals of the Lewis and Clark Expedition;* and Seefeldt, Hantman, and Onuf, *Across the Continent.*

48. Peter S. Onuf and Jeffrey L. Hantman, "Introduction: Geopolitics, Science, and Culture Conflicts," in Seefeldt, Hantman, and Onuf, *Across the Continent,* 1–15; R. J. Miller, "Doctrine of Discovery," 76–103.

49. Seymour I. Schwartz, "Part One," in Schwartz and Ehrenberg, *Mapping of America,* 14–216; Burden, *Mapping of North America,* vol. 2; Conzen and Dillon, *Mapping Manifest Destiny,* 22–51.

50. Osher Map Library and Smith Center for Cartographic Education, "Spaces of Independence: Mapping the Union," in "Mapping the Republic."

51. Schwartz and Ehrenberg, *Mapping of America,* 232–33.

52. Melish, *Geographical Description of the United States,* 4–5.

53. TJ to John Melish, 31 December 1816, ME 15:93. This letter is from the section entitled "Letters Written After His Return to the United States, 1789–1826."

54. J. L. Allen, *Lewis and Clark and the Image of the American Northwest,* 73–108.

55. Edney, "John Mitchell's Map of North

America (1755)," 63–85, "Mitchell Map, 1755–1782," and "Publishing History of John Mitchell's 1755 Map," 4–27 and 71–75.

56. Stein, *Worlds of Thomas Jefferson,* 389–93.

57. Ehrenberg, "Nicholas King," 31–65.

58. *Tooley's Dictionary of Mapmakers* is a useful reference for details regarding a number of early mapmakers and publishers; for additional background on Samuel Lewis, see Ristow, *American Maps and Mapmakers,* 265–66, and Mathews, *Andrew Ellicott.*

59. J. L. Allen, *Lewis and Clark and the Image of the American Northwest,* 74.

60. Albert Gallatin to TJ, 14 March 1803, in Jackson, *Letters of the Lewis and Clark Expedition,* 1:27–28.

61. J. L. Allen, *Lewis and Clark and the Image of the American Northwest,* 78–83; Stein, *Worlds of Thomas Jefferson,* 393.

7. Geographical Miscellanies

1. A number of publications are devoted to Jefferson's expansive scientific interests, including Bedini, *Jefferson and Science* and *Thomas Jefferson: Statesman of Science;* Clagett, *Scientific Jefferson Revealed;* and chapter 2, "Science and the Political Thought of Thomas Jefferson," in Cohen, *Science and the Founding Fathers.* Cohen notes that only one other president of the United States, Theodore Roosevelt, could be considered a potential scientist in politics (61).

2. Schulten, *Geographical Imagination,* 126.

3. Densford, "Educational Philosophy of Thomas Jefferson," 273; Baxter, *Thomas Jefferson and the University of Virginia,* 140. The latter emphasizes that geography was a subject staple as universities began to develop in the early republic. See also Joseph M. Lasala, Patricia C. Sherwood, and Richard Guy Wilson, "Architecture for Education: Jefferson's Design of the Academical Village," in Wilson, *Thomas Jeffer-*

son's *Academical Village,* 1–53. For a general discussion of geography as part of the scaffolding of the general education of a "gentleman," see J. M. Smith, "State Formation," 94–96.

4. TJ, "Commentary and Relevant Extracts . . . ," in *Thomas Jefferson's Farm Book,* has its own contents and pagination, 1–506.

5. TJ, *Thomas Jefferson's Garden Book.* This is presented chronologically from 1766 to 1824 and has a number of appendixes, including "Jefferson's Summary of His Meteorological Journal for the Years 1810 through 1816 at Monticello" (622–28), "The Water Supply at Monticello" (629–31), and "Books and Pamphlets on Agriculture, Gardening, and Botany in the Library of Thomas Jefferson" (655–62).

6. Lehmann-Hartleben, "Thomas Jefferson, Archaeologist."

7. Bedini, *Thomas Jefferson: Statesman of Science,* 105–6. Bedini quotes noted twentieth-century British archaeologist Sir Mortimer Wheeler's admirable comments about Jefferson and his expansive geological and archaeological interests.

8. TJ, *Notes* (1972 ed.), 99–100.

9. Bedini, *Jefferson and Science,* 35–40; Stein, *Worlds of Thomas Jefferson,* 350–63. Although Jefferson had inherited some scientific instruments and a book on astronomy from his father, most of his astronomical equipment was collected beginning with his sojourn to France in 1784. He had intended to leave a portion of his instruments to the University of Virginia. A number survive at Monticello; others, including a valuable equatorial telescope and a Borda circle, cannot be located (Stein, 351).

10. Gilreath and Wilson, *Thomas Jefferson's Library,* chapter 28.

11. Withers, *Placing the Enlightenment,* 195–97. Withers discusses the common contemporary linkage of geographical and astronomical instruction during Jefferson's time, notes that for many eighteenth-century scholars the two subjects were almost indistinguishable, and goes on to discuss specific examples, including the works of Philippe Buache in France and Johann Doppelmaier in Germany.

12. TJ to Joseph Reed, 17 April 1781, *PTJ-D* (http://rotunda.upress.virginia.edu/founders/TSJN-01-05-02-0589); original source *PTJ* 5 (25 February 1781–20 May 1781).

13. TJ to Ezra Stiles, 17 July 1785, *PTJ-D* (http://rotunda.upress.virginia.edu/founders/TSJN-01-08-02-0236); original source *PTJ* 8 (25 February–31 October 1785). Ezra Stiles was a theologian and amateur scientist, and had been involved early in the founding of Brown University. Like other educators of his time, he understood the importance of geographical education.

14. TJ to Bishop James Madison, 29 December 1811, *PTJ-D* (http://rotunda.upress.virginia.edu/founders/TSJN-03-04-02-0283); original source *PTJ-R* 4 (18 June 1811–30 April 1812). More substantive portions of this letter are included in chapter 5, "A Geography of Letters." See the accompanying editorial note in *PTJ-D* regarding the circle of Borda. A meridian, used in this context, is described in that note as "an astronomical instrument consisting of a telescope with a large graduated circle that is used to determine a star's ascension and declination." It is possible that this refers to "Marshall's Meridian Instrument" (see Bedini, *With Compass and Chain,* 305–12), which Jefferson had owned, although no extant example survives.

15. Stephenson and McKee, *Virginia in Maps,* 120–21, 139.

16. TJ to Andrew Ellicott, 24 June 1812, *PTJ-D* (http://rotunda.upress.virginia.edu/founders/TSJN-03-05-02-0137); original source *PTJ-R* 5 (1 May 1812–10 March 1813). As previously mentioned (chapter 5, note 20), Jefferson did

not have access to John Harrison's revolutionary timepiece for the determination of longitude by chronometer (it is not clear he was aware of that advancement, as Harrison's timepieces were scarce and expensive), so most of Jefferson's observations and calculations were predicated on the lunar-distance method, based on the angle between the moon and another celestial body. For a general summary of John Harrison's work and images of several versions of his chronometers, see Royal Museums Greenwich, "John Harrison and the Longitude Problem."

17. TJ, *Notes* (1972 ed.), 19–20.

18. Ibid., 24–25. Jefferson added a footnote on page 264: "Don Ulloa mentions a break, similar to this, in the province of Angaraez, in South America. It is from 16 to 22 feet wide, 111 feet deep, and of 1.3 miles continuance, English measures. Its breadth at top is not sensibly greater than at bottom. But the following fact is remarkable, and will furnish some light for conjecturing the probable origin of our natural bridge . . . Don Ulloa inclines to the opinion, that this channel has been affected by the wearing of the water which runs through it, rather than that the mountain should have been broken open by any convulsion of nature. But if it had been worn by the running of water, would not the rocks which form the sides, have been worn plane? or if, meeting in some parts with veins of harder stone, the water had left prominences on the one side, would not the same cause have sometimes, or perhaps generally, occasioned prominences on the other side also? Yet Don Ulloa tells us, that on the other side there are always corresponding cavities, and that these tally with the prominences so perfectly, that, were the two sides to come together, they would fit in all their indentures, without leaving any void. I think that this does not resemble the effect of running water, but looks rather as if the two sides had parted asunder. The sides of the

break, over which is the Natural bridge of Virginia, consisting of a veiny rock which yields to time, the correspondence between the salient and re-entering inequalities, if it existed at all, has now disappeared. This break has the advantage of the one described by Don Ulloa in its finest circumstance; no portion in that instance having held together, during the separation of the other parts, so as to form a bridge over the Abyss." In this note, Don Ulloa refers to Antonio de Ulloa, a Spanish scientist and member of the French Geodesic Mission to present-day Ecuador for the purpose of measuring the shape of the earth.

19. Hauer, "Thomas Jefferson and the Anglo-Saxon Language," 879.

20. TJ, *Notes* (1972 ed.), 97.

21. Randolph and Francis, "Thomas Jefferson as Meteorologist," 456–58.

22. Lucia S. Goodwin, "Weather Observations," *Thomas Jefferson Encyclopedia,* http://www.monticello.org/site/research-and-collections/weather-observations.

23. TJ, *Garden Book,* 622–28. A Borda circle is a celestial navigational device that was used for surveying during Jefferson's time. More specifically, the device measured the distance between the moon and certain stars as a means of computing longitude. The phrase "nonius divisions" refers to an antecedent of the vernier scale used for distance or angle measurements; these were common on navigational instruments. Jefferson's remarks on climate change were criticized by Noah Webster Jr., although the two never communicated directly about the subject, and Webster's criticisms were more precisely aimed at the speculations of Samuel Williams, author of *The Natural and Civil History of Vermont* (see Kendall, "America's First Great Global Warming Debate").

24. TJ to (New York publisher) George F. Hopkins, 5 September 1822, ME 15:394–95.

25. Dugatkin, *Mr. Jefferson and the Giant Moose,* 62–100. As discussed in therein, Jefferson's contestation of Buffon's theory of American degeneracy, espoused in the latter's *Histoire Naturelle générale et particulière,* went beyond Jefferson's writings in *Notes.*

26. TJ to Joseph Willard, 24 March 1789, *PTJ-D* (http://rotunda.upress.virginia.edu/founders/TSJN-01-14-02-0437); original source *PTJ* 14 (8 October 1788–26 March 1789).

27. TJ to Horatio G. Spafford, 14 May 1809, *PTJ-D* (http://rotunda.upress.virginia.edu/founders/TSJN-03-01-02-0163); original source *PTJ-R* 1 (4 March 1809–15 November 1809). Jefferson owned a copy of Francesco Saverio Clavigero's *Storia antica del Messico,* a well-respected work on the history of Mexico, as well as a number of Constantin-François Volney's works, and Volney was one of his European correspondents.

28. Dugatkin, *Mr. Jefferson and the Giant Moose,* 117.

Epilogue

1. Drake, *Nation's Nature,* 17–66.

2. Redmond, "George Washington: Surveyor and Mapmaker" and "The Mapmaker of Mount Vernon." Washington, with his experience as a public land surveyor and his military surveying in the French and Indian War, was a more technically skilled surveyor than Jefferson. Although Washington had a sizable number of maps and several atlases in his library, they did not match the depth and breadth of Jefferson's holdings in geography and cartography. Washington was more of a land speculator than Jefferson.

3. A. B. Murphy, "Geography's Place in Higher Education," 121, 137–38. With respect to the importance of physical geography in the modern geopolitical landscape, see R. D. Kaplan, *The Revenge of Geography,* 23–37.

BIBLIOGRAPHY

❊ ❊ ❊
❊ ❊
❊

Akerman, James R., ed. *Cartographies of Travel and Navigation.* Chicago: University of Chicago Press, 2006.

Alexander, Sally Kennedy. "A Sketch in the Life of Major Andrew Ellicott." *Records of the Columbia Historical Society* 2 (1899): 158–202.

Allen, Deborah. "Acquiring 'Knowledge of Our Own Continent': Geopolitics, Science, and Jeffersonian Geography, 1783–1803." *Journal of American Studies* 40 (2006): 205–32.

Allen, John Logan. "Imagining the West: The View from Monticello." In *Thomas Jefferson and the Changing West,* edited by James P. Ronda, 3–23. St. Louis: Missouri Historical Society Press, 1997.

———. *Lewis and Clark and the Image of the American Northwest.* New York: Dover Publications, 1991. Originally published as *Passage through the Garden: Lewis and Clark and the Image of the American Northwest* (Urbana: University of Illinois Press, 1975).

———, ed. *North American Exploration.* Vols. 2, *A Continent Defined,* and 3, *A Continent Comprehended.* Lincoln: University of Nebraska Press, 1997.

———. "Thomas Jefferson and the Mountain of Salt: Presidential Image of Louisiana Territory." *Historical Geography* 31 (2003): 9–22.

Anderson, Douglas. "Subterraneous Virginia:

The Ethical Poetics of Thomas Jefferson." *Eighteenth-Century Studies* 33 (2000): 233–49.

Bailyn, Bernard. "Jefferson and the Ambiguities of Freedom." In *To Begin the World Anew: The Genius and Ambiguities of the American Founders,* 37–59. New York: Knopf, 2003.

Baker, Alan R. H. *Geography and History: Bridging the Divide.* Cambridge: Cambridge University Press, 2003.

Banning, Lance, ed. *Liberty and Order: The First American Party Struggle.* Indianapolis: Liberty Fund, 2004.

Baxter, Herbert Adams. *Thomas Jefferson and the University of Virginia.* Washington, D.C.: Government Printing Office, 1888.

Bedini, Silvio A. *Jefferson and Science.* Monticello, Va.: Thomas Jefferson Foundation, 2002.

———. *The Jefferson Stone: Demarcation of the First Prime Meridian of the United States.* Frederick, Md.: Professional Surveyors Publishing Co., 1999.

———. *Thomas Jefferson: Statesman of Science.* New York: Macmillan, 1960.

———. "Thomas Jefferson: Statesman Surveyor." *Professional Surveyor* 13 (1993): 32–39.

———. *With Compass and Chain: Early American Surveyors and Their Instruments.*

Frederick, Md.: Professional Surveyors Publishing Co., 2001.

Bercovitch, Sacvan. *The American Jeremiad*. Madison: University of Wisconsin Press, 1978.

Berg, Scott W. *Grand Avenues: The Story of the French Visionary Who Designed Washington, D.C.* New York: Pantheon Books, 2007.

Berkhofer, Robert F. "Jefferson, the Ordinance of 1784, and the Origins of the American Territorial System." *William and Mary Quarterly* 29 (1972): 231–62.

Berry, Trey. "The Expedition of William Dunbar and George Hunter along the Ouachita River, 1804–1805." *Arkansas Historical Quarterly* 62 (2003): 386–403.

Berry, Trey, Pam Beasley, and Jeanne Clements. *The Forgotten Expedition, 1804–1805: The Louisiana Purchase Journals of Dunbar and Hunter.* Baton Rouge: Louisiana State University Press, 2006.

Betts, Edwin M. "Ground Plans and Prints of the University of Virginia, 1822–1826." *Proceedings of the American Philosophical Society* 90 (1946): 81–90.

Bosse, David. "Institutional Map and Atlas Collecting in Eighteenth-Century America." *Coordinates: Online Journal of the Map and Geography Round Table,* American Library Association, ser. B, no. 9 (17 January 2008), 12. http://purl.oclc.org/coordinates/b9.htm.

Brown, Ralph H. "Jefferson's *Notes on Virginia*." *Geographical Review* 33 (1943): 467–73.

Brückner, Martin. *The Geographic Revolution in Early America: Maps, Literacy, and National Identity.* Chapel Hill: Published for the Omohundro Institute of Early American History and Culture, Williamsburg, Va., by the University of North Carolina Press, 2006.

———. "Lessons in Geography: Maps, Spellers, and Other Grammars of Nationalism in the Early Republic." *American Quarterly* 51 (1999): 311–43.

Burden, Philip D. *The Mapping of North America: A List of Printed Maps.* Vols. 1: 1511–1670 and 2: 1671–1700. Rickmansworth, Herts, UK: Raleigh Publications, 1996/2007.

Cartography Associates. *David Rumsey Map Collection.* Los Angeles: Cartography Associates, 2003. http://davidrumsey.com/index.html.

Casey, Edward S. *Representing Place: Landscape Painting and Maps.* Minneapolis: University of Minnesota Press, 2002.

Cherry, Conrad, ed. *God's New Israel: Religious Interpretations of American Destiny.* Rev. and updated ed. Chapel Hill: University of North Carolina Press, 1998.

Chinard, Gilbert. *Thomas Jefferson: The Apostle of Americanism.* 2nd ed., rev. Ann Arbor: Ann Arbor Paperbacks, University of Michigan Press, 1957.

Clagett, Martin. *Scientific Jefferson Revealed.* Charlottesville: University of Virginia Press, 2009.

Clark, Dan E. "Manifest Destiny and the Pacific." *Pacific Historical Review* 1 (1932): 1–17.

Cohen, I. Bernard. *Science and the Founding Fathers: Science in the Political Thought of Thomas Jefferson, Benjamin Franklin, John Adams, and James Madison.* New York: Norton, 1995.

Cometti, Elizabeth. "Mr. Jefferson Prepares an Itinerary." *Journal of Southern History* 12 (1946): 89–106.

Conzen, Michael P., and Diane Dillon, curators. *Mapping Manifest Destiny: Chicago and the American West.* Chicago: Newberry Library, 2007.

Cosgrove, Denis E. *Geography and Vision: Seeing, Imagining, and Representing the World.* London: I. B. Tauris, 2008.

Cox, Robert S., ed. *The Shortest and Most Convenient Route: Lewis and Clark in Context. Transactions of the American Philosophical Society,* vol. 94, pt. 5. Philadelphia: American Philosophical Society, 2004.

Cunningham, Noble E., Jr. *In Pursuit of Reason: The Life of Thomas Jefferson.* Baton Rouge: Louisiana State University Press, 1987.

Cutright, Paul Russell. *Lewis and Clark: Pioneering Naturalists.* With an introduction by Paul A. Johnsgard. Lincoln: University of Nebraska Press, 2003.

Del Papa, Eugene M. "The Royal Proclamation of 1763: Its Effect upon Virginia Land Companies." *Virginia Magazine of History and Biography* 83 (1975): 406–11.

Densford, John P. "The Educational Philosophy of Thomas Jefferson." *Peabody Journal of Education* 38 (1961): 265–75.

De Vorsey, Louis, Jr. *The Indian Boundary in the Southern Colonies, 1763–1775.* Chapel Hill: University of North Carolina Press, 1961.

Dewey, Frank L. *Thomas Jefferson, Lawyer.* Charlottesville: University Press of Virginia, 1986.

Dion, Leon. "Natural Law and Manifest Destiny in the Era of the American Revolution." *Canadian Journal of Economics and Political Science* 23 (1957): 227–47.

Drake, James D. *The Nation's Nature: How Continental Presumptions Gave Rise to the United States of America.* Charlottesville: University of Virginia Press, 2011.

Dugatkin, Lee Alan. *Mr. Jefferson and the Giant Moose: Natural History in Early America.* Chicago: University of Chicago Press, 2009.

Dunbalin, J. P. D. "Red Lines on Maps: The Impact of Cartographical Errors on the Border between the United States and British North America, 1782–1842." *Imago Mundi* 50 (1998): 105–25.

Dunbar, G. S. "Thomas Jefferson, Geographer." *Special Libraries Association, Geography and Map Division, Bulletin* 40 (1960): 11–16. Reprinted with minor changes and without notes in Dunbar, *The History of Geography: Collected Essays,* 3–7 (Cooperstown, N.Y.: Author, 1996).

Edgerton, Samuel Y., Jr. "Florentine Interest in Ptolemaic Cartography as Background for Renaissance Painting, Architecture, and the Discovery of America." *Journal of the Society of Architectural Historians* 33 (1974): 275–92.

Edney, Matthew M. "John Mitchell's Map of North America (1755): A Study of the Use and Publication of Official Maps in Eighteenth-Century Britain." *Imago Mundi* 60 (2008): 63–85.

———. "The Mitchell Map, 1755–1782: An Irony of Empire." University of Southern Maine: Osher Map Library for Cartographic Education. http://www.oshermaps.org/special-map-exhibits/mitchell-map.

———. "A Publishing History of John Mitchell's 1755 Map of North America." *Cartographic Perspectives* 58 (2007): 4–27 and 71–75.

Ehrenberg, Ralph E. "'Forming a General Geographical Idea of a Country': Mapping Louisiana from 1803 to 1820." In *Charting Louisiana: Five Hundred Years of Maps,* edited by Alfred E. Lemmon, John T. Magill, and Jason R. Wiese (consulting editor John R. Hébert), 123–61. New

Orleans: Historic New Orleans Collection, 2003.

———. "Nicholas King: First Surveyor of the City of Washington, 1803–1812." *Records of the Columbia Historical Society* 69/70 (1969/1970): 31–65.

Ellis, Joseph J. *American Sphinx: The Character of Thomas Jefferson.* New York: Knopf, 1997.

"Envisaging the West: Thomas Jefferson and the Roots of Lewis and Clark." Douglas Seefeldt, project director. University of Nebraska–Lincoln, Center for Digital Research in the Humanities, 2006–7. http://jeffersonswest.unl.edu/.

Fenneman, Nevin M. "The Circumference of Geography." *Geographical Review* 7 (1919): 168–75.

Ferguson, Robert A. "'Mysterious Obligation': Jefferson's Notes on the State of Virginia." *American Literature* 52 (1980): 381–406.

Flores, Dan L., ed. *Southern Counterpart to Lewis and Clark: The Freeman and Custis Expedition of 1806.* Norman: University of Oklahoma Press, 1984.

Friis, Herman R. "A Brief Review of the Development and Status of Geographical and Cartographical Activities of the United States Government: 1776–1818." *Imago Mundi* 19 (1965): 68–80.

———. "Cartographic and Geographical Activities of the Lewis and Clark Expedition." *Journal of the Washington Academy of Sciences* 44 (1954): 338–51.

Gaines, William H., Jr. "An Unpublished Thomas Jefferson Map, with a Petition for the Division of Fluvanna from Albemarle County, 1777." *Papers of the Albemarle County Historical Society* 7 (1946): 23–28.

Ganter, Herbert L. "William Small, Jefferson's Beloved Teacher." *William and Mary Quarterly* 4 (1947): 505–11.

Geography and Map Division, Library of Congress. "Louisiana: European Explorations and the Louisiana Purchase." Library of Congress, updated August 2007. http://memory.loc.gov/ammem/collections/maps/lapurchase/essay1.html.

Gilreath, James. "Sowerby Revirescent and Revised." *Papers of the Bibliographical Society of America* 78 (1984): 219–32.

Gilreath, James, and Douglas L. Wilson. *Thomas Jefferson's Library: A Catalog with Entries in His Own Order.* Washington, D.C.: Library of Congress, 1989. http://catdir.loc.gov/catdir/toc/becites/main/jefferson/88607928.toc.html.

Greenberg, Amy S. *Manifest Manhood and the Antebellum American Empire.* Cambridge: Cambridge University Press, 2005.

Greene, John C. *American Science in the Age of Jefferson.* Ames: Iowa State University Press, 1984.

Hartshorne, Richard. *The Nature of Geography; a Critical Survey of Current Thought in the Light of the Past.* Lancaster, Pa.: Association of American Geographers, 1939.

Hauer, Stanley R. "Thomas Jefferson and the Anglo-Saxon Language." *PMLA* 98 (1983): 879–98.

Hauptman, Laurence M. "Westward the Course of Empire: Geography Schoolbooks and Manifest Destiny, 1783–1893." *Historian* 40 (1978): 423–40.

Hayes, Kevin J. *The Road to Monticello: The Life and Mind of Thomas Jefferson.* Oxford: Oxford University Press, 2008.

Hickisch, Edgar Charles. *Peter Jefferson, Gentleman* (ca. 1949). Special Collections, University of Virginia Library, Charlottesville, accession #MSS 825-a.

Hoffman, John. "Queries Regarding the Western Rivers: An Unpublished Letter from Thomas Jefferson to the Geographer of the United States." *Journal of the Illinois State Historical Society* 75 (1982): 15–28.

Honeywell, Roy J. *The Educational Work of Thomas Jefferson.* Cambridge: Harvard University Press, 1931.

Hubbard, Bill. *American Boundaries: The Nation, the States, the Rectangular Survey.* Chicago: University of Chicago Press, 2009.

Hughes, Sarah S. *Surveyors and Statesmen: Land Measuring in Colonial Virginia.* Richmond: Virginia Surveyors Foundation, 1979.

Hurni, Lorenz, and Gerrit Sell. "Cartography and Architecture: Interplay between Reality and Fiction." *Cartographic Journal* 46 (2009): 323–32.

Jackson, Donald, ed. *Letters of the Lewis and Clark Expedition, with Related Documents, 1783–1854,* 2nd ed., with additional documents and notes. 2 vols. Urbana: University of Illinois Press, 1998.

———. *Thomas Jefferson and the Stony Mountains: Exploring the West from Monticello.* Urbana: University of Illinois Press, 1981.

Jefferson, Thomas. "An Account of Louisiana," 14 November 1803. *American State Papers: Miscellaneous,* vol. 1. Document No. 164, 1st Session, 8th Congress.

———. *The Jeffersonian Cyclopedia; A Comprehensive Collection of the Views of Thomas Jefferson.* Edited by John P. Foley. New York: Funk and Wagnalls Company, 1900.

———. *Jefferson's Memorandum Books: Accounts, with Legal Records and Miscellany, 1767–1826.* Edited by James Adam Bear and Lucia C. Stanton. Princeton: Princeton University Press, 1997.

———. "Letters." Charlottesville: Electronic Text Center, University of Virginia, 1993.

http://etext.virginia.edu/toc/modeng/public/JefLett.html.

———. *Message from the President of the United States, Communicating Discoveries Made in Exploring the Missouri, Red River, and Washita, by Captains Lewis and Clark, Doctor Sibley, and Mr. Dunbar; with a Statistical Account of the Countries Adjacent.* New York: Hopkins and Seymour, 1806; facsimile edition at http://www.americanjourneys.org/aj-090/.

———. *Notes on the State of Virginia.* London: J. Stockdale, 1787. http://etext.virginia.edu/toc/modeng/public/JefVirg.html.

———. *Notes on the State of Virginia.* Edited with an introduction and notes by William Peden. New York: Norton Library (published by arrangement with University of North Carolina Press), 1972.

———. *The Papers of Thomas Jefferson.* Edited by Julian Boyd. 39 vols. to date. Princeton: Princeton University Press, 1950–.

———. *The Papers of Thomas Jefferson Digital Edition.* Edited by Barbara B. Oberg and J. Jefferson Looney. Charlottesville: University of Virginia Press, Rotunda, 2008.

———. *The Papers of Thomas Jefferson, Retirement Series.* 9 vols. to date. Edited by J. Jefferson Looney. Princeton: Princeton University Press, 2004–.

———. *Thomas Jefferson, Architect: Original Designs in the Coolidge Collection of the Massachusetts Historical Society.* With an essay and notes by Fiske Kimball, and a new introduction by F. D. Nichols. New York: Da Capo Press, 1968.

———. *Thomas Jefferson's Farm Book: With Commentary and Relevant Extracts from Other Writings.* Edited by Edwin Morris Betts. Chapel Hill: University of North Carolina Press, 2002.

———. *Thomas Jefferson's Garden Book, 1766–1824: With Relevant Extracts from His Other Writings.* Annotated by Edwin Morris Betts. Charlottesville: Thomas Jefferson Memorial Foundation, 1999.

———. *The Works of Thomas Jefferson.* 12 vols. Collected and edited by Paul Leicester Ford. New York: G. P. Putnam's Sons, 1904–5.

———. *The Writings of Thomas Jefferson.* 20 vols. Edited by Andrew A. Lipscomb and Albert Ellery Bergh. Washington, D.C.: Thomas Jefferson Memorial Association of the United States, 1903–4.

Jefferson, Thomas, and William Dunbar. *Documents Relating to the Purchase and Exploration of Louisiana.* 2 parts. Boston: Houghton Mifflin, 1904.

"The John Adams Library at the Boston Public Library." Boston Public Library. http://www.johnadamslibrary.org/.

Johnston, William Dawson. *History of the Library of Congress: Volume I, 1800–1864.* Washington, D.C.: Government Printing Office, 1904.

Kain, J. P. Roger, and Elizabeth Baigent. *The Cadastral Map in the Service of the State: A History of Property Mapping.* Chicago: University of Chicago Press, 1992.

Kaplan, Lawrence S. *Thomas Jefferson: Westward the Course of Empire.* Wilmington: SR Books, 1999.

Kaplan, Robert D. *The Revenge of Geography: What the Map Tells Us About Coming Conflicts and the Battle Against Fate.* New York: Random House, 2012.

Katz, Stanley N. "Thomas Jefferson and the Right to Property in Revolutionary America." *Journal of Law and Economics* 19 (1976): 467–88.

Kellner, Charlotte. *Alexander von Humboldt.* New York: Oxford University Press, 1963.

Kendall, Joshua. "America's First Great Global Warming Debate." Smithsonian.com, http://www.smithsonianmag.com/history-archaeology/Americas-First-Great-Global-Warming-Debate.html.

Kite, Elizabeth S. *L'Enfant and Washington 1791–1792: Published and Unpublished Documents Now Brought Together for the First Time.* Baltimore: Johns Hopkins Press, 1929.

Koelsch, William A. "Thomas Jefferson, American Geographers, and the Uses of Geography." *Geographical Review* 98 (2008): 260–79.

Kraus, Joe W. "Private Libraries in Colonial America." *Journal of Library History* 9 (1974): 31–53.

Kukla, Jon. *A Wilderness So Immense: The Louisiana Purchase and the Destiny of America.* New York: Knopf, 2003.

Lambeth, W. A., and Warren H. Manning. *Thomas Jefferson as an Architect and a Designer of Landscapes.* New York: Houghton Mifflin, 1913.

Lawson-Peebles, Robert. *Landscape and Written Expression in Revolutionary America: The World Turned Upside Down.* Cambridge: Cambridge University Press, 1988.

Ledyard, John. *Journey through Russia and Siberia, 1787–1788: The Journal and Selected Letters.* Edited with an introduction by Stephen D. Watrous. Madison: University of Wisconsin Press, 1966.

Lehmann-Hartleben, Karl. "Thomas Jefferson, Archaeologist." *American Journal of Archaeology* 47 (1943): 161–63.

Lemmon, Alfred E., John T. Magill, and Jason R. Wiese, eds., with John R. Hébert, consulting ed. *Charting Louisiana: Five Hundred Years of Maps.* New Orleans: Historic New Orleans Collection, 2003.

Lewis, Anthony Marc. "Jefferson and Virginia's pioneers, 1774–1781." *Mississippi Valley Historical Review* 34 (1948): 551–88.

Lewis, Jan, and Peter S. Onuf. "American Synecdoche: Thomas Jefferson as Image, Icon, Character, and Self." *American Historical Review* 103 (1998): 125–36.

Lewis, Meriwether, and William Clark. *The Journals of the Lewis and Clark Expedition*, 13 vols. Annotated set, edited by Gary E. Moulton. Lincoln: University of Nebraska Press, 2002.

Library of Congress, Geography and Map Division. *American Memory: Maps Collections*. Washington, D.C.: Library of Congress. http://memory.loc.gov/ammem/browse/ListSome.php?category=Maps.

———. *American Memory: A Century of Lawmaking for a New Nation, U.S. Congressional Documents and Debates*. Washington, D.C.: Library of Congress. http://memory.loc.gov/ammem/amlaw/lawhome.html.

———. *Rivers, Edens, Empires: Lewis and Clark and the Revealing of America*. Washington, D.C.: Library of Congress. http://www.loc.gov/exhibits/lewisandclark/lewisandclark.html.

———. *Thomas Jefferson's Library: A Catalog with the Entries in His Own Order*. Edited by James Gilreath and Douglas L. Wilson. Washington, D.C.: Library of Congress, 1989 (reproduced 2001). http://catdir.loc.gov/catdir/toc/becites/main/jefferson/88607928.toc.html.

Linklater, Andro. *Measuring America: How an Untamed Wilderness Shaped the United States and Fulfilled the Promise of Democracy*. New York: Walker, 2002.

Looney, J. Jefferson. "Thomas Jefferson: Practical Scientist." *Journal of the Pennsylvania Academy of Science* 67 (1993): 94–99.

Lowenthal, David, and Martyn J. Bowden, eds. *Geographies of the Mind: Essays in Historical Geosophy In Honor of John Kirtland Wright*. Oxford: Oxford University Press, 1975.

Malone, Dumas. *Jefferson and His Time*. 6 vols. Boston: Little, Brown, 1948–81.

Mapp, Paul W. *The Elusive West and the Contest for Empire, 1713–1763*. Chapel Hill: Published for the Omohundro Institute of Early American History and Culture, Williamsburg, Va., by the University of North Carolina Press, 2011.

Mathews, Catharine Van Cortlandt. *Andrew Ellicott: His Life and Letters*. New York: Grafton Press, 1908.

Mayhew, Robert J. "Geography in Eighteenth-Century British Education." *Paedagogica Historica* 34 (1998): 731–69.

McCormick, Richard P. "The 'Ordinance' of 1784?" *William and Mary Quarterly* 50 (1993): 112–22.

McDonald, Robert M. S., ed. *Thomas Jefferson's Military Academy: Founding West Point*. Charlottesville: University of Virginia Press, 2004.

Meinig, D. W. *Atlantic America, 1492–1800*. Vol. 1 of *The Shaping of America: A Geographical Perspective on 500 Years of History*. New Haven: Yale University Press, 1986.

———. *Continental America, 1800–1867*. Vol. 2 of *The Shaping of America: A Geographical Perspective on 500 Years of History*. New Haven: Yale University Press, 1993.

Melish, John. *Geographical Description of the United States, with the contiguous British and Spanish Possessions, intended as an accompaniment to Melish's Map of these Countries*. Philadelphia: Author, 1816.

Reprinted by Williams Printing Company, Nashville, 1972.

Miller, Iris. *Washington in Maps 1606–2000.* New York: Rizzoli International Publications, 2002.

Miller, Robert J. "The Doctrine of Discovery in American Indian Law." *Idaho Law Review* 42 (2005): 76–103.

———. *Native America, Discovered and Conquered: Thomas Jefferson, Lewis and Clark, and Manifest Destiny.* Westport: Praeger, 2006.

Monmonier, Mark. *Drawing the Line: Tales of Maps and Cartocontroversy.* New York: Henry Holt, 1995.

Morgan, Edmund S. "The Chosen People." In *The Genuine Article: A Historian Looks at Early America,* 31–39. New York: Norton, 2004.

———. "Thomas Jefferson." In *The Meaning of Independence: John Adams, George Washington, and Thomas Jefferson,* 61–87. Charlottesville: University Press of Virginia, 1976.

Morse, Jedidiah. *The American Geography; or, A View of the Present Situation of the United States of America.* Elizabeth Town: Shepard Kollock, 1789.

Murphy, Alexander B. "Geography's Place in Higher Education in the United States." *Journal of Geography in Higher Education* 31 (2007): 121–41. http://geography.uoregon .edu/murphy/articles/murphy_jghe_ manuscript%20with%20figures.pdf.

Murphy, Mark. "The Natural Law Tradition in Ethics." *The Stanford Encyclopedia of Philosophy* (Fall 2008), edited by Edward N. Zalta. http://plato.stanford.edu/archives/ fall2008/entries/natural-law-ethics/.

Nichols, Frederick Doveton, and Ralph E. Griswold. *Thomas Jefferson, Landscape Architect.* Charlottesville: University Press of Virginia, 1978.

Nobles, Gregory H. "Straight Lines and Stability: Mapping the Political Frontier." *Journal of American History* 80 (1993): 9–35.

Ogburn, Floyd, Jr. "Structure and Meaning in Thomas Jefferson's Notes on the State of Virginia." *Early American Literature* 15 (1980): 141–50.

Onuf, Peter S. *Jefferson's Empire: The Language of American Nationhood.* Charlottesville: University Press of Virginia, 2000.

Osborn, H. F. "Thomas Jefferson as a Paleontologist." *Science Magazine* 82 (1935): 533–38.

Osher Map Library and Smith Center for Cartographic Education. "Mapping the Republic: Conflicting Concepts of the Territory and Character of the U.S.A., 1790–1900." University of Southern Maine: Osher Map Library & Smith Center for Cartographic Education, 15 May 2003–29 May 2004. http://www.oshermaps.org/ exhibitions/mapping-republic.

O'Sullivan, John L. "Annexation." *The United States Democratic Review* 17 (1845): 5–10. http://digital.library.cornell.edu/cgi/t/text/ text-idx?c=usde;cc=usde;view=toc;subview =short;idno=usde0017-1.

Oswald, Michael J., and R. John Moore. "The Mapping of Architectural and Cartographic Faults: Troping the Proper and the Significance of (Coast) Lines." *Architectural Theory Review* 3 (1998): 1–22.

Owsley, Frank Lawrence, Jr., and Gene A. Smith. *Filibusters and Expansionists: Jeffersonian Manifest Destiny, 1800–1821.* Tuscaloosa: University of Alabama Press, 1997.

Padover, Saul K., ed. *Thomas Jefferson and the National Capital: Containing Notes and*

Correspondence Exchanged Between Jefferson, Washington, L'Enfant, Ellicott, Hallet, Thornton, Latrobe, the Commissioners, and Others, Relating to the Founding, Surveying, Planning, Designing, Constructing, and Administering of the City of Washington, 1783–1818. Washington, D.C.: Government Printing Office, 1946.

Pattison, William D. "The Four Traditions of Geography." *Journal of Geography* 89 (1990): 202–6.

Peden, William. "Some Notes Concerning Thomas Jefferson's Libraries." *William and Mary Quarterly,* 3rd ser., vol. 1, no. 3 (July 1944): 265–72.

Pedley, Mary Sponberg. *The Commerce of Cartography: Making and Marketing Maps in Eighteenth-Century France and England.* Chicago: University of Chicago Press, 2005.

Peterson, Merrill D., ed. *Thomas Jefferson: A Reference Biography.* New York: Scribner, 1986.

Pollak, Martha. "Military Architecture and Cartography in the Design of the Early Modern City." In *Envisioning the City: Six Studies in Urban Cartography,* edited by David Buisseret, 109–24. Chicago: University of Chicago Press, 1998.

Pratt, Joseph Hyde. "American Prime Meridians." *Geographical Review* 32 (1942): 233–44.

Pratt, Julius W. "The Origin of 'Manifest Destiny.'" *American Historical Review* 32 (1927): 795–98.

Price, Edward T. *Dividing the Land: Early American Beginnings of Our Private Property Mosaic.* Chicago: University of Chicago Press, 1995.

Randolph, Fred. J., and Fred. L. Francis. "Thomas Jefferson as Meteorologist." *Monthly Weather Review* 23 (1895): 456–58.

Raphael, Henry. "Thomas Jefferson, Astronomer." *Astronomical Society of the Pacific,* leaflet no. 174 (August 1943): 184–91.

Rebok, Sandra. "Enlightened Correspondents." *Virginia Magazine of History and Biography* 116 (2008): 329–69.

———. *Humboldt and Jefferson: A Transatlantic Friendship of the Enlightenment.* Charlottesville: University of Virginia Press, 2014.

Redmond, Edward. "George Washington: Surveyor and Mapmaker." Washington, D.C.: Library of Congress. http://memory.loc.gov/ammem/gmdhtml/gwmaps.html.

———. "The Mapmaker of Mount Vernon." *The Early American Review* 10 (Winter/Spring 2001). http://www.earlyamerica.com/review/2001_winter_spring/mapmaker_mv.html.

Reinhold, Meyer. "The Quest for 'Useful Knowledge' in Eighteenth-Century America." *Proceedings of the American Philosophical Society* 119 (1975): 108–32.

Reps, John. *Washington on View: The Nation's Capital Since 1790.* Chapel Hill: University of North Carolina Press, 1991.

Ristow, Walter W. *American Maps and Mapmakers: Commercial Cartography in the Nineteenth Century.* Detroit: Wayne State University Press, 1985.

Ronda, James P. *Astoria and Empire.* Lincoln: University of Nebraska Press, 1990.

———. "Dreams and Discoveries: Exploring the American West, 1760–1815." *William and Mary Quarterly* 46 (1989): 145–62.

———. "'A Knowledge of Distant Parts': The Shaping of the Lewis and Clark Expedition." *Montana: The Magazine of Western History* 41 (Autumn 1991): 4–19.

———. *Thomas Jefferson and the Changing West.* St. Louis: Missouri Historical Society Press, 1997.

———. "'To Acquire What Knoledge You Can': Thomas Jefferson as Exploration Patron and Planner." *Proceedings of the American Philosophical Society* 150 (2006): 409–13.

Royal Museums Greenwich. "John Harrison and the Longitude Problem." http://www.rmg.co.uk/explore/astronomy-and-time/time-facts/harrison.

Salisbury, Neal. "Red Puritans: The 'Praying Indians' of Massachusetts Bay and John Eliot." *William and Mary Quarterly,* 3rd ser., 31 (1974): 27–54.

Schöpflin, George, and Geoffrey A. Hosking, eds. *Myths and Nationhood.* New York: Routledge, 1997.

Schulten, Susan. *The Geographical Imagination in America, 1880–1950.* Chicago: University of Chicago Press, 2001.

Schwartz, Seymour I., and Ralph E. Ehrenberg. *The Mapping of America.* New York: Abrams, 1980.

Schwarz, Ingo. "Alexander Von Humboldt's Visit to Washington and Philadelphia, His Friendship with Jefferson, and His Fascination with the United States." *Northeastern Naturalist,* special issue 1 (2001): 43–56.

Scott, Donald M. "The Religious Origins of Manifest Destiny." Divining America, TeacherServe. National Humanities Center, rev. December 2008. http://nationalhumanitiescenter.org/tserve/nineteen/nkeyinfo/mandestiny.htm.

Seefeldt, Douglas, Jeffrey L. Hantman, and Peter S. Onuf, eds. *Across the Continent: Jefferson, Lewis and Clark, and the Making of America.* Charlottesville: University of Virginia Press, 2005.

Shalev, Eran. "'A Perfect Republic': The Mosaic Constitution in Revolutionary New England, 1775–1788." *New England Quarterly* 82 (2009): 235–63.

Short, John Rennie. *Representing the Republic: Mapping the United States, 1600–1900.* London: Reaktion Books, 2001.

Smart, George K. "Private Libraries in Colonial Virginia." *American Literature* 10 (1938): 24–52.

Smith, Ben A., and James W. Vining. *American Geographers, 1784–1812: A Bio-Bibliographical Guide.* Westport: Praeger, 2003.

Smith, Jonathan M. "State Formation, Geography, and a Gentleman's Education." *Geographical Review* 86 (1996): 91–100.

Sorrenson, Richard. "The Ship as a Scientific Instrument in the Eighteenth Century." *Osiris, 2nd Series, Science in the Field* 11 (1996): 221–36.

Sowerby, E. Millicent. *Catalog of the Library of Thomas Jefferson.* 5 vols. Washington, D.C.: Library of Congress, 1952–59.

Staloff, Daren. *Hamilton, Adams, Jefferson: The Politics of Enlightenment and the American Founding.* New York: Hill and Wang, 2005.

Stanley, William A. "Ferdinand R. Hassler—Survey of the US Coast 1807–1843." *IMCoS Journal* 115 (2008): 17–23.

Stein, Susan R. *The Worlds of Thomas Jefferson at Monticello.* New York: Abrams, 1993.

Stephanson, Anders. *Manifest Destiny: American Expansion and the Empire of Right.* New York: Hill and Wang, 1995.

Stephenson, Richard W. *A Plan Whol[l]y New: Pierre Charles L'Enfant's Plan of the City of Washington.* Washington, D.C.: Library of Congress, 1993.

Stephenson, Richard W., and Marianne M. McKee. *Virginia in Maps: Four Centuries of Settlement, Growth, and Development.* Richmond: Library of Virginia, 2000.

Stockdale, Eric. *'Tis Treason My Good Man!: Four Revolutionary Presidents and a Picadilly Bookshop.* New Castle: Oak Knoll Press, 2005.

Strauss, Leo. *Natural Right and History.* Chicago: University of Chicago Press, 1953.

Surface, George Thomas. "Thomas Jefferson: A Pioneer Student of American Geography." *Bulletin of the American Geographical Society* 41 (1909): 743–50.

Terra, Helmut de. "Alexander von Humboldt's Correspondence with Jefferson, Madison, and Gallatin." *Proceedings of the American Philosophical Society* 103 (1959): 783–806.

Theberge, Captain Albert E. *The Coast Survey 1807–1867.* Vol. 1 of the *History of the Commissioned Corps of the National Oceanic and Atmospheric Administration.* http://www.lib.noaa.gov/noaainfo/heritage/coastsurveyvol1/CONTENTS.html.

"Thomas Jefferson's Libraries." Monticello, Va.: Thomas Jefferson Foundation. http://tjlibraries.monticello.org/.

Tooley, R. V. *Tooley's Dictionary of Mapmakers,* 4 vols. Rev. ed., edited by Josephine French, Mary Alice Lowenthal, and Valerie Scott. Tring, Herts, UK, and Riverside, Conn.: Map Collector Publications and Early World Press, 1999–2004.

Verner, Coolie. "The Fry and Jefferson Map." *Imago Mundi* (1967) 21: 70–94.

———. "The Maps and Plates Appearing with the Several Editions of Mr. Jefferson's 'Notes on the State of Virginia.'" *Virginia Historical Magazine* 59 (1951): 21–53.

———. "Mr. Jefferson Makes a Map." *Imago Mundi* (1959) 14: 96–108.

Volo, James M., and Dorothy Denneen Volo. *Family Life in Seventeenth- and Eighteenth-Century America.* Santa Barbara: Greenwood Press, 2005.

Wallace, Anthony F. C. *Jefferson and the Indians: The Tragic Fate of the First Americans.* Boston: Belknap Press, 1999.

Walls, Laura Dassow. *The Passage to Cosmos: Alexander von Humboldt and the Shaping of America.* Chicago: University of Chicago Press, 2009.

Warner, Deborah Jean. "True North—and Why It Mattered—in Eighteenth Century America." *Proceedings of the American Philosophical Society* 149 (2005): 372–85.

Weeks, William Earl. *Building the Continental Empire: American Expansion from the Revolution to the Civil War.* Chicago: Ivan R. Dee, 1996.

Weinberg, Albert K. *Manifest Destiny: A Study of Nationalist Expansion in American History.* Baltimore: Johns Hopkins Press, 1935.

Wheat, Carl I. *Mapping the Transmississippi West, 1540–1861.* Reprint ed., 5 vols. in 6. Storrs-Mansfield: Maurizio Martino Publisher, 1995.

Williams, Charlie. "Explorer, Botanist, Courier, or Spy? André Michaux and the Genet Affair of 1793." *Castanea: Occasional Papers in Eastern Botany,* Proceedings of the Andre Michaux International Symposium, edited by Michael J. Baranski, 98–106. Southern Appalachian Botanical Society, 2006.

Williams, Glyndwr. *Voyages of Delusion: The Quest for the Northwest Passage.* New Haven: Yale University Press, 2003.

Wilson, Douglas L. *Jefferson's Books.* Monticello, Va.: Thomas Jefferson Foundation, 1996.

———. "Sowerby Revisited: The Unfinished Catalog of Thomas Jefferson's Library." *William and Mary Quarterly* 41 (1984): 615–28.

———. "Thomas Jefferson's Library and the

French Connection." *Eighteenth-Century Studies* 26 (1993): 669–85.

Wilson, Richard Guy, ed. *Thomas Jefferson's Academical Village: The Creation of an Architectural Masterpiece.* Rev. ed. Charlottesville: University of Virginia Press, 2009.

Winthrop, John. "A Modell of Christian Charity (1630)." *Collections of the Massachusetts Historical Society,* 3rd ser., vol. 7 (1838): 31–48.

Withers, Charles W. J. "Eighteenth-Century Geography: Texts, Practices, Sites." *Progress in Human Geography* 30 (2006): 711–29.

———. *Placing the Enlightenment: Thinking Geographically about the Age of Reason.* Chicago: University of Chicago Press, 2007.

Wooldridge, William C. *Mapping Virginia: From the Age of Exploration to the Civil War.* Charlottesville: Published for the Library of the Mariners' Museum by the University of Virginia Press in association with the Virginia Cartographical Society, 2012.

Woolery, William Kirk. *The Relation of Thomas Jefferson to American Foreign Policy, 1783–1793.* St. Clair Shores: Scholarly Press, 1971.

Worms, Laurence, and Ashley Baynton-Williams. *British Map Engravers: A Dictionary of Engravers, Lithographers and Their Principal Employers to 1850.* London: Rare Book Society, 2011.

INDEX

❈ ❈ ❈
❈ ❈
❈

Italicized page numbers refer to illustrations.

Claiborne, William C. C., 119
Clark, Daniel, Jr., 119
Clark, George Rogers, 56, 57, 93–95
Clark, William, 4, 55, 93, 128; *A Map of Lewis and Clark's Track*, 126–27, 128. *See also* Lewis and Clark expedition
Clavigero, Francesco Saverio, 141, 165n27
climate, 35–37, 104, 105, 138–40
climate change, 37, 139, 164n23
coasts, surveying of, 5, 17
College of William and Mary, 11, 106, 159n37
compasses, 13, *14*
Cook, James, 3, 37, 55, 60, 124
correspondence, 6, 86–110
counties of Virginia, 38. *See also* Albemarle County (Va.); Fluvanna County (Va.)
Coxe, Trent, 17
Cruz Cano, Juan de la, 1
Custis, Peter, 79, 83–84

Davis, William, 135
de Brahm, John William Gerard, 13
de Bry, Theodore, 153n16
Delahaye, Guillaume, 39
Delisle, Guillaume, 61, 124, 155n31; *Carte de la Louisiane et du Cours du Mississipi*, 64, *74–75*, 128
Dictionary of the English Language, A (Johnson), 3, 146n9
Discovery, Right of. *See* Right of Discovery
Doctrine of Discovery. *See* Right of Discovery
Donelson, John, 10
Dunbar, William, 4, 79–83, 102–5, 119, 159n31
Dunbar-Hunter expedition, 4, 79–83, 102–5; *Map of the Washita river in Louisiana* (King), *80–81*, 83

Ebeling, Christoph Daniel, 86–87, 107, 144
education: in astronomy, 131, 132, 163n11; in engineering, 59; in geography, 5, 31, 130, 131, 143, 144, 162n3, 163n11; in surveying, 9, 11
Elizabeth I (Queen), 38
Ellicott, Andrew, 6, 17, 18–20, 60, 97–98, 99–102, 124, 128, 133–34, 144, 148n30; *Plan of the City of Washington in the territory of Columbia*, 20, *24–25*
engineering education, 59
Enlightenment, the, 3, 86
equatorial telescopes, 13, 133, 163n9
Evans, Lewis, 34; *A general Map of the middle British colonies in America*, *46–47*, 48
expedition planning: Louisiana Purchase, 4, 65–85, 102–3, 117, 118–20, 143; Pacific Northwest, 4, 55–64, 79, 83, 94–95, 101–2, 106, 120–21, 143. *See also* Dunbar-Hunter expedition; Freeman-Custis expedition; Lewis and Clark expedition; Right of Discovery
"Eye Draught of Madison's Cave, An" (T. Jefferson), 35, *36*

Faden, William, 39; *The North American Atlas*, 39
Farm Book (T. Jefferson), 130
Fluvanna County (Va.), *12, 13*
Fontaine, Peter, 10
Franklin, Benjamin, 139, 144
Freeman, Thomas, 79, 83–84
Freeman-Custis expedition, 79, 83–84; *Map of the Red River in Louisiana* (King), 84–85, *84–85*
Fry, Joshua, 10; *A Map of the most Inhabited part of Virginia*, 1, 10, 34, 39, *42–43*, 48, 151–52n30

Gallatin, Albert, 17, 60–62, 64, 118, 128, 144
Garden Book (T. Jefferson), 131, 163n5
Garrett, John, 148n30
Gates, Horatio, 88
general Map of the middle British colonies in America, A (Evans), *46–47*, 48
Genêt, Edmond-Charles, 59
Geographical Description of the United States with the continuous British and Spanish Possessions (Melish), 124
geography: definition of, 3–4, 130; education in, 5, 31, 130, 131, 143, 144, 162n3, 163n11; and the Enlightenment, 3; and Manifest Destiny,

112; as "mother of all sciences," 3, 130, 142, 143; textual vs. visual, 5, 146n19
Georgia, 116–17
Great Library (T. Jefferson's), 3, 4, 5, 50–54, 59, 131, 143, 147n24, 152n1, 152n8, 155n27
Gunter's chain, 13

Hamilton, Alexander, 1, 18
Harrison, John, 158n20, 164n16
Hartley, David, 16, 148n25
Harvie, John, 17
Hassler, Ferdinand Rudolph, 17
Hennepin, Louis, 78
Henry VIII (King), 4
Homann, Johann Baptist, 79, 120, 155n31, 161n43
Hopkinson, Francis, 48
Humboldt, Alexander von, 6, 86, 105–6, 113, 144, 159n36; *Carte Generale Du Royaume De La Nouvelle Espagne, 82, 84*
Hunter, George, 4, 79–83, 102, 156n34
Hutchins, Thomas, 89–90, 107; *A New Map of the Western Parts of Virginia, Pennsylvania, Maryland, and North Carolina, 44, 48; A Topographical Description of Virginia, Pennsylvania, Maryland, and North Carolina, 89–90*

Inter caetera (1493), 115

Jay, John, 57
Jefferson, Peter (T. Jefferson's father), 4, 10, 147n4, 152n9; *A Map of the most Inhabited part of Virginia, 1, 10, 34, 39, 42–43, 48, 151–52n30*
Jefferson, Thomas (T. Jefferson's great-grandfather), 10
Jefferson, Thomas: *Account of Louisiana,* 119; and agriculture, 130–31; and archaeology, 131; and astronomy, 11, 106–7, 131–33, 163n9; on cities, 18, 149n32; correspondence of, 6, 86–110; education of, 11, 130, 143; "An Eye Draught of Madison's Cave," 35, *36; Farm Book,* 130; *Garden Book,* 131, 163n5;

Great Library of, 3, 4, 5, 50–54, 59, 131, 143, 147n24, 152n1, 152n8, 155n27; legal career of, 10, 11–13, 116, 143; and linguistics, 102–3, 104–5, 138; and the Louisiana Purchase, 4, 65–85, 102–3, 117, 118–20, 143; and Manifest Destiny, 111–29; *A Map of the country between Albemarle Sound and Lake Erie, 2,* 38–49; and meteorology, 35–37, 104, 105, 138–40; and the Pacific Northwest, 4, 55–64, 79, 83, 94–95, 101–2, 106, 117, 120–21, 143; and planning of the University of Virginia, 6, 20–29, 143; and planning of Washington, D.C., 18–20, 143; scientific instruments of, 10, 11, 13–15, *14,* 107, 133, 139, 163n9, 163n14, 164n23; surveying interests of, 5, 9–29, 131–32; unpublished map of proposed creation of Albemarle County from Fluvanna County, *12,* 13; and "useful knowledge," 4, 11, 59; varied interests of, 1, 130. *See also* Monticello (Va.); *Notes on the State of Virginia* (T. Jefferson)
Jefferson-Hartley map, 148n25
Jefferys, Thomas, maps in *The American Atlas,* 39; *An Accurate Map of North and South Carolina, 45; A Map of Pennsylvania, 40–41; A Map of the most Inhabited part of Virginia, 42–43*
Johnson, Samuel, *A Dictionary of the English Language,* 3, 146n9
Johnson v. M'Intosh, 114
Joliet, Louis, 65, 78

King, Nicholas, 17, 20, 124–28, 144, 148n30, 155n20; Lewis and Clark base map, 60–61, 64, *66–67,* 128; *Map of the Red River in Louisiana, 84–85, 84–85; Map of the Washita river in Louisiana, 80–81, 83*
Kirby, Ephraim, 119

Lafayette, Gilbert du Motier, Marquis de, 88–89, 157n9
Lambert, William, 106, 107, 133
land charters, 9
land ownership, 115–17. *See also* Manifest Destiny

landscape, 4, 112

Lapérouse, Jean-François de Galaup, Comte de, 57, 154n7

La Salle, René-Robert Cavalier, Sieur de, 78, 109

Latin School, 11

Latrobe, Benjamin Henry, 20, 29, 149n41

Ledyard, John, 56–57

L'Enfant, Pierre Charles, 6, 18–20, 97–99, 149n36; *Plan of the city intended for the permanent seat of the government of t[he] United States*, 20, 22–23

letters. *See* correspondence

Lewis, Meriwether, 4, 55, 60–61, 62, 63, 81, 99, 101–2, 108, 120, 128, 148n30. *See also* Lewis and Clark expedition

Lewis, Samuel, 128; *Louisiana*, *125*, 128; *A Map of Lewis and Clark's Track*, 126–27, 128

Lewis and Clark base map (King), 60–61, 64, 66–67, 128

Lewis and Clark expedition, 4, 55, 60–64, 79, 83, 101–2, 106, 117, 120–21, 124–28, 154n14

Library of Congress, 5, 50, 51, 52, 147n24

linguistics, 102–3, 104–5, 138

Locke, John, 117

longitude, determination of, 95–97, 100–101, 133–36, 158n20, 164n16, 164n23

Louis XVI (King), 57

Louisiana (S. Lewis), *125*, 128

Louisiana Purchase, 4, 65–85, 102–3, 117, 118–20, 143

Luzerne, Anne-César, Chevalier de la, 89

Mackenzie, Alexander, 55, 61, 62, 124, 144; *A Map of America*, 64, *72–73*; *Voyages from Montreal*, 55, 153n2

Madison, James (Bishop), 6, 106–7, 133, 135, 144, 159n37; *A Map of Virginia Formed from Actual Surveys*, 1, 133, *134–35*, 159n37, 160n40

Madison, James (President), 13, 18, 90–93, 114, 148n30

Madison's Cave, 35, *36*

magnetic declination, 106

Manifest Destiny, 111–29; biblical roots of, 114; and geography, 112; and the Lewis and Clark expedition, 120–21; and the Louisiana Purchase, 118–20; mapping of, 108, 121–29; and natural law, 117–18; origin of the phrase, 112; and Right of Discovery, 114–17

Mansfield, Jared, 17

Map Exhibiting all the New Discoveries in the Interior Parts of North America, A (Arrowsmith), 64, *68–69*, 118, 128

Map of America, A (Mackenzie), 64, *72–73*

Map of Lewis and Clark's Track, A (S. Lewis), *126–27*, 128

Map of Pennsylvania, A (Jefferys), 39, *40–41*

Map of the British and French Dominions in North America, A (Mitchell), 64, *76–77*, 124, 128

Map of the country between Albemarle Sound and Lake Erie, A (T. Jefferson), 2, *38–49*

Map of the most Inhabited part of Virginia, A (Fry-Jefferson), 1, 10, 34, 39, *42–43*, 48, 151–52n30

Map of the Red River in Louisiana (King), 84–85, *84–85*

Map of the United States of North America, A (Arrowsmith), 64, *70–71*, 128

Map of the United States with the contiguous British and Spanish Possessions (Melish), 108, 121, *122–23*, 124

Map of the Washita river in Louisiana (King), *80–81*, 83

Map of Virginia Formed from Actual Surveys, A (Bishop Madison), 1, 133, *134–35*, 159n37, 160n40

maps: for boundary disputes, 4; cartography as a word, 3, 145n5; for Lewis and Clark expedition, 60–61, 64, 124–28; for Louisiana Territory, 78–85, 118–20; and Manifest Destiny, 108, 121–29; as way-finding devices, 4, 145n5. *See also individual maps by title*

Marbois, François, 5, 30, 89, 118, 146–47n21, 150n3, 150n7

Marquette, Jacques, 65, 78

Marshall's Meridian Instrument, 11, 13, 163n14

Martin, Alexander, 16
Mason, George, 116
Mather, Cotton, 51, 152n4
Maury, James, 11
Maverick, Peter, plan of the University of
Virginia, 28
Mayo, William, 10
Melish, John, 107–10, 121, 124, 160n41; *Geo-
graphical Description of the United States with
the continuous British and Spanish Posses-
sions,* 124; *Map of the United States with the
contiguous British and Spanish Possessions,*
108, 121, *122–23,* 124; *Travels in the United
States of America,* 107–8
meridians (scientific instruments), 11, 13, 107,
163n14
meridians, prime. *See* prime meridians
meteorology, 21, 35–37, 104, 105, 138–40
Mexico, 105–6
Michaux, André, 58–59
minerals, 35
M'Intosh, Johnson v., 114
Mitchell, John, 61, 124; *A Map of the British
and French Dominions in North America,* 64,
76–77, 124, 128, 155n23
Moll, Herman, 79, 120, 155n31, 161n43
Monroe, James, 114
Montesquieu, 117
Montgomery, Cora. *See* Cazneau, Jane McMa-
nus Storm
Monticello (Va.): agriculture at, 130; design of,
20–21, 87, 143; entrance hall at, 1, 4, 124, 128;
first version plan by T. Jefferson, *26;* longi-
tude of, 106–7; mountaintop layout plan by
T. Jefferson, *27*
Moore, Joshua, 148n30
Morse, Jedidiah, 30, 86; *The American
Geography,* 30, 150nn5–6
mountains, 33–34
Mouzon, Henry, 48

Native Americans: archaeological remains of,
131; and land-claim disputes, 116–17; languages of, 102–3, 104–5, 138; and the Loui-
siana Purchase, 118; and Right of Discovery,
115, 116–17; in Virginia, 37–38, 131
Natural Bridge (Va.), 136, 137–38, 142, 164n18
natural history, 35, 103, 140–41. See also *Notes
on the State of Virginia* (T. Jefferson)
natural law, 117–18
Neele, Samuel, 39
*New Map of the Western Parts of Virginia, Penn-
sylvania, Maryland, and North Carolina, A*
(Hutchins), *44,* 48
New Spain, 105–6
North American Atlas, The (Faden), 39
Northwest Passage, 56, 57, 120
Northwest Territory, 16, 90–93, 148n25
Notes on the State of Virginia (T. Jefferson), 30–
49; on boundaries, 31–33; on cascades, 34–35;
on caves, 35, *36;* as a chorography, 5, 136–39;
on climate, 35–37; contents page of, *32;* on
counties, 38; "An Eye Draught of Madison's
Cave," 35, *36;* as a geographical treatise, 30,
150n4; *A Map of the country between Albemarle Sound and Lake Erie,* 38–49; on minerals, plants, and animals, 35; on mountains,
33–34, 136–37; on Native Americans, 37–38,
131; on Natural Bridge, 136, 137–38, 142,
164n18; origins of, 5, 30, 89, 118, 146–47n21;
on passage of the Potomac River through the
Blue Ridge Mountains, 136–37, 141; on population, 37; on ports, 33; on Walter Raleigh,
38, 141; response to, 30, 87, 150n3; on rivers,
33, 136–37, 141; unpublished sketches in
Jefferson's copy of, 151n16

O'Sullivan, John L., 112

Pacific Northwest, 4, 55–64, 83, 94–95, 101–2,
106, 117, 120–21, 143, 146n11
Page, John, 21, 48
Patterson, Robert, 148n30
Penn, William, 33
Pennsylvania, 13, 132
Pennsylvania Mutiny, 18
perambulators, 13
Petty, William, 157n7; *Survey of Ireland,* 88

Voltaire, 1
Voyages from Montreal (Mackenzie), 55, 153n2;
   A Map of America, 64, 72–73

Washington, George, 16, 58, 92–93; and planning of Washington, D.C., 18, 97, 98–99;
   surveying skills of, 144, 147n11, 165n2
Washington, D.C.: planning of, 18–20, 87,
   97–100, 143; *Plan of the city intended for the
   permanent seat of the government of t[he]
   United States* (L'Enfant), 20, 22–23; *Plan
   of the City of Washington in the territory of
   Columbia* (Ellicott), 24–25

Webster, Noah, Jr., 37, 151n19, 164n23
West Point (N.Y.), 59
White, Alexander, 88
Wilkinson, James, 79
Willard, Joseph, 140
Williams, Samuel, 164n23
winds, 105
written itineraries, 4, 145n5

Zach, Franz Xaver, 159n38
Zimmerman, 141